THE MULTICULTURAL CURRICULUM

Education in a Multicultural Society

Series Editor: Maurice Craft
Professor of Education
University of Nottingham

Further titles in preparation:

LANGUAGE IN MULTICULTURAL CLASSROOMS
Viv Edwards

HOME, SCHOOL AND COMMUNITY
Sally Tomlinson

The Multicultural Curriculum

James Lynch

Batsford Academic and Educational Ltd
London

Typeset by Progress Filmsetting Ltd
and printed in Great Britain by
Billing & Sons Ltd.
Worcester
for the publishers
Batsford Academic and Educational Ltd
4 Fitzhardinge Street
London W1H 0AH

British Library Cataloguing in Publication
Data
Lynch, James
The multicultural curriculum.
1. Education—Great Britain—Curriculum
I. Title
375'.008'0941   LB1564.G7

ISBN 0 7134 4510 6

Contents

Acknowledgements 6

Editor's preface 7

1 Multicultural education: the context and the case 9

2 The teacher and multicultural education 24

3 A framework for a multicultural curriculum 55

4 The community and the multicultural school 84

5 Resources for multicultural curriculum development: an introductory overview 102

6 The multicultural curriculum: some guidelines for action 119

Notes and references 130

Select bibliography 144

Index 152

Acknowledgments

I should like to express my sincere appreciation to the many teachers, administrators and academics and to my colleagues, past and present, whose thoughts and writings have contributed so much to the 'making' of this book. I also owe a substantial debt to the multicultural city in which I grew up, for what I now realize was a unique opportunity to experience a multicultural education in practice.

I should also like to thank those authors and publishers who have kindly given permission for the reproduction in this text of copyright material, as follows: Professor James Banks and the National Council for the Social Studies for the chart on p.49 reprinted from James A. Banks, 'Ethnic Studies as a Process of Curriculum Reform', *Social Education* (1976), vol. 40, p.78; Her Majesty's Stationery Office for permission to quote from the Consultative Document *Education in Schools* (1977) and *The School Curriculum* (1981); Dr. Brian Bullivant and Macmillan Australia for permission to reproduce Figure Eight from Dr. Bullivant's book *Race, Ethnicity and Curriculum* (Melbourne: Macmillan, 1981). Figure Three on p.51 has been reproduced from Curriculum Development Centre, *A Core Curriculum for Australian Schools* (Canberra: CDC, 1980).

A particular word of thanks is due to many colleagues in the United States, Canada and Australia whose work has fundamentally influenced and broadened my understanding of what multicultural education means. I have tried to take account of their work in what I have written. To the editor of this series, Professor Maurice Craft, and the Senior Editor of Batsford, Mr Anthony Seward, I extend my warm appreciation for their confidence in the idea of the book and for their assistance in its completion. To Susan Holliday goes credit for the speedy, patient and accurate typing and re-typing of the manuscript and to Caryl Sutcliffe warm thanks for the preparation of the index. Finally, a special word of gratitude is due to my wife, Margaret, for her assistance with some of the interviews in Australia, the United States and Canada, which provided invaluable material for the book, and, as always, for her irreplaceable and unrelenting support and enthusiastic encouragement.

James Lynch
Ilkley, September 1982

Editor's Preface

It is now coming to be more widely recognised that Britain is a culturally diverse society, and has been for centuries. Variations of belief and behaviour according to region, religion, class and ethnicity have always existed, but we are now increasingly conscious of the greater potential for enrichment – as well as for conflict – that these variations make possible. This new series will seek to explore some of the more salient educational issues presented by cultural diversity, and with particular reference to *ethnicity*. It will aim to contribute to the skills and understanding of teachers, teacher trainers, educational administrators and policymakers, whose concern is to provide for the educational needs of all children growing up in a multicultural society.

The *Multicultural Curriculum* is the first title to appear, and has been written by Professor James Lynch who draws on his extensive experience of work in this field here and overseas. The shape of the school curriculum in a multicultural and multi-ethnic society is a central but particularly complex question, and Professor Lynch seeks to map both its philosophical and its practical dimensions. Other titles will consider related aspects of education for all children in a multicultural Britain.

Maurice Craft
University of Nottingham

1 Multicultural education: the context and the case

'Multicultural education' is simply a convenient shorthand term used in discussing the concept of 'education for a multicultural society'. It can only arise in such a society and be embedded within that particular ethical context. It is necessary, therefore, first to identify the underlying ethic of a multicultural society before decisions and policies for its educational system can be proposed. Only then can discussion commence as to what kind of curriculum might be appropriate for schools.

Hence, this first chapter begins with a description of how and why the United Kingdom of the 1980s may be described as a multicultural society, and what I mean by that statement. The underlying principles of that society are then identified and I argue that a commitment to the concept of a multicultural society necessarily commits advocates of an education appropriate to it, to those principles underlying it. My major purpose in this chapter is to suggest that these principles are the basic means whereby rational, 'person-respecting' decisions can be taken about the selection of valued knowledge that we call curriculum.

In what ways is the United Kingdom a multicultural society?

But firstly, in what ways is the United Kingdom a multicultural society? Is it unique in this respect? And, has it only more recently become one? In any case, how does the concept 'multicultural' relate to similar ones in use at the moment, such as 'multiracial', 'polyethnic', 'multicredal', 'bilingual', 'bicultural', etc?

The term 'multicultural' may be considered to embrace and go beyond all the above terms. They are more restricted in meaning – perhaps even more precise, but they are also exclusive of important cultural groups in our society. Take 'multiracial', for example. This refers to the existence within one social system (it may be the nation state) of several different races: caucasoid, negroid, etc. (Examples of such societies would include Australia, Fiji, Singapore, the United States and, of course, the United Kingdom). We are certainly a multiracial society and we must make sure that our educational system educates for racial harmony and against racial bigotry and discrimination. But we are more than that, for we are also a multicredal society and a multiethnic society, that is, we have peoples of many different faiths and religious beliefs, and none, who should all command our respect. Moreover, we have peoples who are descended from different ethnic groups, from the Celts, the Romans and the Normans to the Jews, Poles, Irish and Vietnamese of more recent settlement. We also have people who are bilingual by birth or later acquisition of a second language and many who are functional in more than one culture. All of these different cultural groups merit respect and it is therefore important that the description which we use for our society makes it clear that this is so for all legitimate cultural groups and not just for some. It is for this reason that I use the term multicultural as a comprehensive descriptor of our society which embraces the multiracial, multicredal, multiethnic and multicultural composition of that society.

Given that the United Kingdom is a multicultural society, then all else should flow from that: its laws, its institutions, its schooling and its curriculum. So the question of whether our society has always been multicultural and whether other societies are such is academic, for the contemporary fact is that we are one now. That said, it will be clear from what has been written above that we have been a multicultural society for a long time and that other countries have as well. The fact that our perception (and theirs) has only more recently become sharpened towards a greater recognition of that fact merely indicates the dislocation which has been taking place between education and society, for which a reconceived multicultural education and curriculum must now seek to correct.

So, in a sense, contemporary British society is not unique in time or space in being multicultural. It has always been multicultural – and at no period more markedly so than since the Industrial Revolution – and many other societies around the globe are multicultural too. So we can learn from each other in building multicultural education.

Within our society, there have always been different groups which have felt a social or economic affinity that has resulted in their establishing a patterned network of human relations, and which has meant that they have thereby begun to generate and transmit cultural values and meanings. These values and meanings may have overlapped with those of other groups, but they were also clearly distinguishable from them and from those of the dominant groups of the time. At the same time, it is indisputable that English education has tended to give preferential treatment to the needs of predominant groups in society to secure the economic and political systems. This has often resulted in flight by other legitimate groups from the mainstream education which was offered, as in the case of the non-comformist Academies of the eighteenth century, the proprietary schools of the nineteenth and the alternative schools of the twentieth.

But the substantial demographic changes of the post-Second World War period coincided with a period of renewed emphasis on individualism and the pursuit of equality of opportunity, which caused a fundamental reappraisal. Influences from countries abroad too, such as the United States, have meant that assimilationist 'melting pot' approaches to social organization, cultural transmission and educational opportunity could no longer be justified amongst the population at large as far as the average teacher is concerned. Rather the reverse, for the pendulum in the United States has swung from the attempt to impose a false unity (false because for some it had to be a segregated unity), through the intergroup and intercultural movements of the 1940s to the rampant cultural pluralism of the 1960s and back again to a concept somewhere between the two. That concept has been variously described, amongst other things, as multicultural and multiethnic.

In this book the term 'multicultural education' is used as going beyond multiracial or multiethnic education. It embraces them both, and other concepts such as multicredal and bilingual education, but it is less exclusive. Thus, while the change to a manifestly multicultural society is more recent in the United Kingdom, the movement to recognize British society as multicultural is part of an older continuity!

Regardless of when they occur, however, such changes in the racial or cultural composition of a society (or more precisely the increased recognition of them) make heavy demands on all members of that society, and these demands are more acutely felt in the very fulcrum of cultural transmission, the schools and other education establishments. As one infant school's policy statement succinctly puts it:

1. The school is multicultural and all that goes on within it must strive to reflect and build upon this basis;
2. Culture is central to a child's identity, and the learning environment must reflect the cultures of those learning within it and *within society at large* [my italics];
3. Teachers must become aware of the cultures from which children come and the customs and attitudes within them...?

It is in the schools that the newly changed perceptions of the cultural mosaic of society have to be translated against the background of the rhetoric of politicians and educationists alike into the arena of decision and action. This is not to suggest either a linear process or autonomy on the part of the school, for it is clear that schools interact with, influence and are influenced by the broader society. The quotation above seems to me to allow for this. The point is that changed perceptions in the wider society pose imperatives for schools, to which they must respond, but that these imperatives are usually indistinct, oblique and hazy, sometimes illogical and contradictory.

For example, the newer commitment to multicultural education has to be measured against the over-riding commitment of education in any society to secure social cohesion. Clearly, society would fall apart if this were not the case. Thus, education has to prepare us to recognize that we are alike, as for example, members of one species, but different as well, in sex, social class, religion, culture, competence and expertise: infinite in diversity but united in our humanity.

The resultant dilemma has been called by Bullivant 'the pluralist dilemma'.[?] Essentially, Bullivant is drawing attention to the conflict between celebrating pluralism and maintaining social cohesion, to the basic contradiction of an education aimed at both diversity and unity. He might have added that, in a country such as the United Kingdom, the apparent unity in education is, in any case, a mirage, for there are many systems: for example, the Public School System and the state system, and within both there is and has been a hierarchy and differentiation according to social class, academic achievement, religion, sex, age, etc.

Each of the social groups which provides the clientele for such schools strives to perpetuate its concept of the most important values, meanings and knowledge, not only as the content of contemporary education, but as the determinant of future decisions about education and learning. Thus, at the same time the content of education is both substance and criteria: criteria for future substance but also for determining what is valued culture in society at large, and even more importantly what cultural capital will lead to economic wellbeing and advancement. It will thus be used as a means to influence access to power and resources in society.

What is the culture in multiculturalism?
Crudely stated, it is precisely because culture influences life chances as well as life styles, and is the central concept of 'multiculturalism' in

education, that we need to define more closely what we mean by culture – before we can then proceed to define multicultural education. Be warned! There are many competing definitions of culture and no final agreement, and many advocates of multicultural education in the United States have argued that established definitions of culture must not be allowed to dictate the meaning of multiculturalism and that it would be premature to be too firm about definitions. But, it seems to me, we have to know, at least roughly, what it is we are debating. So, as a tentative working definition only, what I mean by culture in this book is a network of values, conceptions, methods of thinking and communicating, customs and sentiments (for it is not wholly rational) used as a socio-ecological coping mechanism by individuals, groups and nations.[4] It is an active capital of non-material, socio-historical character which attracts 'compound interest' in interaction with the social and natural environment so as to secure the survival of the individual and the group. All accretions to the culture are achieved through the 'good offices' of the existing capital.

Societies, which are in practice territorially defined political units, consider their cultural 'capital' so valuable that they establish special agencies to preserve, supervise and transmit 'valued' selections to all new members of society: a process which is called enculturation. In nation states much of this process of cultural transmission is entrusted to formal institutions called schools. But how do they do this? What channels do they use? For Hirst and Peters, the transmission of valued knowledge is achieved through clearly distinguishable forms of knowledge, which coincide more or less with established academic disciplines, and which are fundamental to the development of rationability and thus to being educated.[5] For others, including myself, such a view has led to an unbalanced selection of valued knowledge. Rationality, according to this view, is subject to social negotiation and would be enhanced through the pursuit of a new 'common culture' which was more socially and regionally representative, pluralist and open, and intellectually reflexive. Note, I am not denying the contemporary importance of forms of knowledge, merely arguing that they are not 'the whole story'. I am concerned, however, that there should be greater awareness of the significance of the development of shared meanings through greater social co-operation, balance and therefore equality within a multicultural society.

Jeffcoate argues that a broader, less elitist and less ethnocentric definition of a common culture (and a common curriculum no doubt) requires just such a reflexive, critical 'revaluation' as an established feature of British society and of British education? For this purpose, he envisages the school as filling the function of social critic and cultural synthesizer. Such a function would certainly be compatible with the overall functions of education in a democratic society but would place a heavier burden on them (and on teachers) than at present. It would, for instance, presuppose the existence of a set of publicly negotiated rational criteria against which contending cultural capital could be sifted and sorted for inclusion in 'school knowledge'. Likewise, it would presuppose a greater dialogue between school and community than has currently been achieved, and perhaps a realignment of our thinking on schooling towards an acceptance of Peters's view that the summit of moral development is the ability to reflect upon the principles which guide our actions? And herein, to my view, lies the nearest we shall attain to identifying, defining, utilizing and refining categorical 'imperatives' to guide opinion, value and action in a multicultural society.

But let us get back for a moment to the question of the selection of knowledge. The alternative to selection, namely a totally random, *en bloc* absorption of all cultural capital projected in the direction of the school, would clearly be both illogical and unacceptable, for it would inevitably imply the inclusion of anti-social capital and very rapidly lead to breakdown through overload. As Zec points out, respect for the richness and strengths of culture (and their inclusion in that valued selection which we call curriculum) presupposes evaluative criteria which he calls generalizable maxims? Only thus, he argues, can cultural diversity be reconciled with objectivity and universality as a basis for a worthwhile multicultural education for which we need to know, to use Leach's words, 'how things are related, not just how they can be taken apart'?

How can knowledge be selected for multicultural education?

It will be clear from what has been said above that a 'soft, folksy tokenism' approach to multicultural education, where all cultural values and meanings of all cultural groups are supposed to be equally acceptable merely because they are different, is not tenable. Such a concept of multicultural education can become so diffuse that it actually blurs rather than clarifying elements, dissipating resource utilization and mushrooming to the point where it means everything to everyone. Such an intellectual position would be neither rational nor likely to be educational in its outcomes. Not only would the resulting educational policy be unlikely to succeed, (for in the educational progression that is life, those who had restricted their educational intake to the functional, the rational and the educational would once again come off best, thus defeating the whole purpose of multicultural education, namely the pursuit of greater cultural respect and equality of educational opportunity, pursued through one's own legitimate culture), but it would also be a practical impossibility.

It must be apparent, moreover, that not all cultural values are of equal worth. To give but one example, the practice of mutilating young girl children, prevalent and practised in some cultural groups, would never be generally acceptable as a norm for (or to) the whole of British society. The practice of some minority political groups of deliberately inciting racial hatred (of groups for instance such as the Ku Klux Klan in the United States) could not be acceptable. Nor would these two examples of cultural deviance even be acceptable as rationally founded and thus explicitly sanctioned norms for a constituent group of a society such as ours which propagates equality of the sexes, the integrity of the individual, an abhorrence of violence towards children, and racial tolerance. In the inevitable and irreconcilable clash in these cases between the rational 'universals' and the sometimes irrational particulars of a cultural group, the 'universals' must surely hold sway.

The reader will no doubt have noticed that a key, if implicit, factor in this argument is that the particular requires the rational universal for its legitimation. Let me explain what I mean by that. The exploration and evaluation of local knowledge, both geographical and cultural, can only take place judged against something which has a wider validity, what I am going to call for the moment 'the universals'. It is only in terms of these latter that exploration and evaluation can take place, and moreover, a society without shared universals would disintegrate. In short, multicultural education does not mean, indeed cannot mean, that everything and anything goes, but it does offer a more objective, open and deliberate means of deciding what goes within a multicultural society.

Such considerations need not, however, be inimical to the kind of more critical and evaluative role and the greater autonomy for the multicultural school, which Jeffcoate is advancing. Indeed they can enhance such a role. For, ideally, multicultural education can be considered as the initiation of children into critical-rational acceptance of cultural diversity and the creative affirmation of individual and group difference within a common humanity. That means that it is a process conducted according to explicit, rational evaluative criteria: an ethical process, celebrating both diversity and unity, social differentiation and cohesion, stability and deliberate, systematic and evaluated change according to explicit yardsticks, themselves the subject of critical discourse.

What kind of criteria could be used?

But what would these evaluative criteria be and who would decide which criteria should be included and which not, and when they might become redundant? This is a sensitive, controversial and difficult question which has remained largely unaddressed by advocates of multicultural education.[10] Yet it is central to the development of a realistic and functional multicultural education within a modern, industrial market economy and society that is tolerant, humane and politically relatively stable. Education, in brief, and therefore the school curriculum, has to look to the good of the community, to the provision of economic health and to the freedom and creativity of the individual. It has to prepare children to take their places in society as citizens, as workers and consumers, and as creative persons, working for its progression and change. Since fulfilling a range of different functions, social, political and economic, presupposes institutionalized preparation for such roles – in schools or other educational institutions – the school needs to be functionally related to but not dominated by such functions.

Cultural capital unrelated to that functionality by open, objective and rational criteria would be redundant or superfluous and, whilst such culture would be available for preservation at the individual or small group level, according to criteria of the 'gradation of functionality', it would have a low claim to inclusion in the valued cultural capital that we call curriculum. This may sound hard, but once it is conceded that not all cultural capital can be included in curriculum, the fact of selection has to be faced as has also the continuing social viability of knowledge and therefore its redundancy. As the allegory of the 'sabre-tooth curriculum' implies, it is possible for previously highly functional knowledge to become degraded and even redundant, a phenomenon which has occured in our own time in the movement from imperial weights, measures and currency to decimal systems.[11]

A multicultural society is particularly demanding in regard to the selection of valued cultural capital, both because of the richness of capital 'on offer' and because it requires respect and tolerance for the culture of others, which in turn demands cultural overlap to an extent which is necessary for effective knowledge, understanding and inter-communication. To make way for that common ground, and because there is a limit to the capital which can comprise a curriculum, a hierarchy of functionality, rationality and universality has to be identified. These we might call the meta-values or criteria for knowledge sorting and sifting. We shall return to this point shortly, but for the moment let us review where we have got to so far.

To summarize, British society of the twentieth century is a multicultural society, not just a multicredal or multiethnic one. Such a society necessitates a multicultural education and a corresponding curriculum. A curriculum based on total absorption of all available cultural capital is non-viable, however, because:

a. it would result in overload;
b. not all culture is equally worthy and therefore acceptable;
c. culture needs to be adaptive and functional (if only in the interests of the survival of the species);
d. it would not allow for sufficient overlap or common ground to secure social cohesion.

It follows that selection is necessary from the available cultural (actually multicultural) capital, and that process of selection in turn points to the need for criteria against which such a selection can take place, and mechanisms for the generation and consideration of criteria and their practical application. As I suggested earlier, such criteria might be typified, in a kind of shorthand, as concerning the functions of an individual in society as a person, as a worker and as a citizen and they could be 'tempered' by some means of assessing their rationality, objectivity and universality.[12] These considerations would then yield a grid of reflexive and adaptive criteria (see Figure 1).

Figure 1
SOCIAL CRITERIA FOR THE SELECTION OF KNOWLEDGE

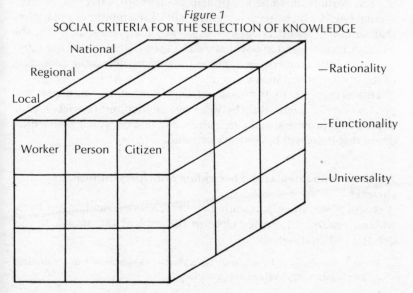

The opposites of these criteria would be subjectivity, particularism and primordiality or assumed givenness, yielding a continuum where the locus of the criteria would be different according to the level involved – for example, person, worker or citizen, at local, regional or national levels – and, of course, the age range of children or learners concerned.[13] Potentially at least, the criteria must allow for interplay and mutual influence between the major social imperatives that constitute our contemporary society – democracy, industralization and individualism (citizen, worker, private person) – whilst at the same time offering some measure of both continuity and pluralism, both culturally and geographically. Thus, whilst there are certain overarching economic activities of our society as a whole, there are also regional and local variations, such as textile manufacture in the West Riding, coal mining in Durham, shipbuilding on the Tyne. Similarly, although there are certain universals that are functionally necessary for all members of our society, for example, command of English, commitment to democracy and the rule of law, this does not rule out the presence of regional or local languages, local by-laws and the like. Indeed commitment to pluralist democracy cannot so rule them out. But why not, you may ask, seen theoretically and philosophically at least?

In embryo, this question touches on the question of the ethic of the multicultural society. Let us for a moment pause to look behind the social criteria which have been suggested and ask whether there are, in fact, certain fundamental principles – perhaps universal, or even eternal ones – which are so integral a part of the multicultural society that without them it could not exist. For I am conscious that the social criteria suggested could as well be used to perpetuate the *status quo,* with little concern for a tolerant pluralism, unless the core ethic of society contained such a commitment.

This brings me to the most difficult part of my own personal position on the relationship between our multicultural society and its educational provision and curriculum, and one on which I have little doubt that there will be contrary opinions.

Are there fundamental and overriding principles intrinsic to society?

A recent government publication on the school curriculum, probably without realizing it, comes close to the core of the answer to this question, when it states,

> What is taught in schools, and the way it is taught, must appropriately reflect fundamental values in our society.[14]

Admittedly, the document then goes on to identify the fact that British society has become multicultural as an 'issue', rather than a principle or a value or an imperative or an ethic out of which certain kinds of decision about education and curriculum automatically flow. But even given that the document also made a mess of the statement of aims which it contains,[15] the above question does provide an important touchstone for our theme, because behind it (implicitly and amongst other issues), as also behind the functionally identified criteria proposed above, hovers, I suggest, the question as to the availability of fundamental principles which could be used as reference points to decisions concerning what kind of multicultural education is appropriate to our society. Put another way, is there a yardstick for the application of the social criteria? Further, are there, for instance, certain basic ethical principles which could serve this purpose for all cultures?

The answer to the last question is probably a qualified 'no', in the sense that, it could be argued, there do exist principles which are basic to the 'Western European Ethic'. Multicultural societies are an extension of that ethic and its fundamental principle of respect for persons, out of which our democratic institutions and major political concepts such as equality, freedom and justice are derived.[16] Multicultural education is the education appropriate for a multicultural society, and as the London Borough of Brent states in its approach to the issue, 'Multicultural education and education cannot be seen as separate entities in a fair and just society'.[17] Commitment to a multicultural society thus necessarily commits one to the ethical principles underlying that society, and coincidentally it also rules out practices which run counter to those principles on the grounds that commitment to the 'ethic' is logically prior.

Additionally, if the 'multicultural educator' is committed to an ethical state at all, then it is to the principles underlying a multicultural society in Britain, to the principles mentioned above, and for both of these reasons to 'respect for persons'.[18] An understanding of how this principle works out in our democratic institutions and political concepts is crucial to the stability and continuing viability of a multicultural society. Moreover, although understanding is necessary, it is not sufficient as a basis for decision and action appropriate to a multicultural society, because the important momentum to the construction and perpetuation of such a society is given by the behaviour which flows from these principles. But in what sense is it possible to decide on behaviour which is congruent with these principles and therefore with the aims and ethic of a multicultural society?

Although it is not uncontroversial, it seems to me that the work of Wilson *et al.* offers some way forward in response to that question. He has suggested several principles which must govern opinions before they can be classified as moral opinions, namely they must be autonomous, that is, subject to free will; rational; impartial, as between persons; prescriptive for all, including the individual; and overriding, in the sense of taking precedence over the person's other opinions.[19] The absence of any of the principles would render the opinion non-moral, and the same applies to action. On the other hand, the presence of all might not guarantee morality but render it subject to what I have called discourse.[20]

It will perhaps be clear that the third principle, impartiality, implies a concern for other people's interests which may be seen as extensions of one's own. All of these principles, but particularly the third and fourth, imply, as Wilson points out, accepting others on an equal footing to ourselves: a respect for persons that is fundamental to western society and institutional concepts, as it must be to any multicultural society. Moreover, the very fact that the principles include mutual prescriptiveness means that there must be an equality of application: that any action we take must contain our acceptance of its equal applicability to ourselves.

Without going into the minutiae of the argument, it is from such principles that criteria for 'moral' opinions and actions, that is, behaviour congruent with the ethic of a multicultural society, may be derived, and it is from them that fundamental concepts and institutions of western democratic society are drawn in turn. Against them also can be measured the social criteria for decisions about the aims of education and the content of valued knowledge that we call a curriculum, all of which may be appropriate to a multicultural society. This complex process is neither linear nor does it exclude the central role of discourse. Rather it seeks to emphasize the importance of communicative competence amongst all cultural groups and individuals in society as an essential pre-requisite to that discourse, which will secure a functional and 'culturally fair' inclusion of content in the curriculum of a multicultural school. In that sense and with minor amendments, Jeffcoate's enunciation of respect for others as one of the major objectives dominant in multicultural education, is correct?[21] But this is a topic which will be dealt with in greater detail later.

What kind of overall curriculum structure does the above argument imply?

For the moment, it is necessary to ask what kind of overall

curriculum structure may fulfil the need to select in a balanced way from the available multiculture of modern British society, whilst at the same time securing the economic and political mainstays of that society and offering respect for persons and their cultures. In other words, what kind of curriculum in outline, and what kinds of strategies put into operation the principles, criteria and processes that I have suggested in the first part of this chapter? Put differently, having briefly considered the Why?, what are the implications for the What? of education, that is, the curriculum?

All the above three areas, personal, economic and political, must be addressed for all children, irrespective of their regional or cultural background, or they will not be able to take a full place in society. The consequence of neglect of any one would probably be the collapse of the kind of multicultural, industrial and democratic society for which we are seeking to educate. But, in addition, the principle of respect for persons would appear to require the representation, in some way or other, of all legitimate (in terms of that society's ethic) cultures for all of the population, for knowledge and awareness are prerequisites to respect and it is illogical to expect respect without any grounding of knowledge. Thus a kind of 'knowledge chart' of our multicultural society is an essential for all members of that society. There are other essentials too, which I shall deal with in later chapters, but for the present this one example suffices to illustrate my argument. Now such a chart might not be universally considered to be directly functional in terms of the 'worker' criterion suggested above. Its inclusion might not be capable of justification by reference to the vocational aims of education, necessary in our industrial and technological society. It might even (for some) be debatable whether it would be functional in terms of the 'citizen' criterion: it might not relate necessarily to the need in a democracy for articulate and participating, politically aware voter-members of society. (I believe that it does). But it could certainly be functional in terms of the 'person' criterion and the underlying principle of respect for persons discussed above, potentially expressing both individualism (and to some extent intrinsic aims for education) and creative momentum for change in society (that is, extrinsic aims for the individual addressed to the good of others).

The logic of this argument leads to the tailoring of such common elements into a curriculum related functionally to the 'person', 'worker', 'citizen' paradigm for all children, with extras, alternates, options or choices which might be more closely but not exclusively related to the 'person' dimension. And what is valid for the 'person' criterion is also valid for the 'worker' dimension, bearing in mind differential human abilities and regional distinctions and differences in the industrial and economic bases: vocational and cultural options in other words, attached to a common core curriculum, according to cultural and geographical location, and influenced of course by age-range, need and cognitive style.

But before deploying that argument more fully in later chapters, I would here return to my point about the role of discourse in the whole process of deciding the why, what, how and where of education, and the need for greater dialogue between school and society and school and community. For in a democratic and open society, such decisions cannot be subject to *Diktat*. This process is neither linear nor mechanistic but subject to the 'bonfire night bombardment' of oral, visual, aural and other stimuli, although, perhaps, slightly less predictable!

How can the necessary discourse be achieved?

The process of building an education and a curriculum appropriate to a multicultural society like ours is not to be thought of solely in terms of content and structures. Rather, respect for others implies respect for their opinions and beliefs and willingness to engage in dialogue about them and the appropriate aim of education in that society. All of this adds up to the need to cherish dialogue between individuals and groups across the whole range of our social 'credos' and institutions. If we are indeed to have a humane multicultural society then individuals and institutions must know how to engage in such dialogue and be willing to do so.

I am aware that the extent to which the school has done this so far is very limited. But there are very welcome signs of change with the whole thrust of the teacher self-evaluation movement,[22] the new Schools Council Programme orientation (and the publication of *The Practical Curriculum*[23]) and, perhaps also implicitly, with the imperatives of recent publications and Circulars from the Department of Education and Science. There is certainly a healthy current concern with accountability and monitoring although I shall argue the need later for this to be broadened and deepened, if multicultural education is to be achieved. More, the process of discussion will necessarily need to include a more balanced distribution of influence between school and community and between lay, professional, political and administrative members of society than it currently does. It will also incidentally need to include the recognition that grown-ups do not have a monopoly of rationality nor children of emotionality, and that this recognition will need to embrace an acknowledgement of the way children can, and apparently do, take responsibility for their own and their peers' learning.[24]

For the moment, having briefly mapped out the field, let us consider what multicultural education implies for the teacher and what efforts have already been made in different and diverse places to design and implement a multicultural curriculum, before returning in Chapter Four to the need for greater discourse and its role in the construction of a multicultural curriculum.

Summary
This chapter has:
1. suggested that recognizing the United Kingdom as a multi-cultural society presents social and ethical imperatives for education and the curriculum;
2. offered a working definition of culture as a basis for under-standing multicultural education;
3. outlined a typology for social criteria to select knowledge in a multicultural society;
4. argued the presence of overriding principles to facilitate educational decisions and policy;
5. suggested that the implementation of a curriculum according to the above criteria and principles implies greater discourse in society at large and particularly between school and community;
6. promised, in the next chapter, some ideas on what multicultural education may mean for teachers and some examples of multicultural curricula.

2 The teacher and multicultural education

In Chapter One I emphasized the rather more theoretical stages in the necessary process of systematically and rationally building up a multicultural curriculum, which will permit of cultural diversity whilst maintaining a commitment to social cohesion. Some of my readers may be bridling at this and asking for more concrete fare which will help them to construct such a curriculum. How, they may ask, given the ethical and social imperatives suggested in Chapter One, does the greater recognition of the need for multicultural education affect me and are there any examples of multicultural curricula from which I can learn? What does it mean for me and how can I learn from what other people have done in the field? This chapter gives consideration to both of these fundamental and important questions, so let us see where they take us.

The challenge of cultural diversity
The potential ramifications for the teacher of the challenge of cultural diversity are truly huge, and to try to get some initial purchase on them, I intend to introduce the rather controversial concept of 'assimilation' as a means of showing how different cultural groups, and therefore different pupils, stand in what I shall term a different relationship to 'traditional British culture' as represented within contemporary school values, knowledge, and teaching methods than do others. I must hasten to say that I am not seeking to justify the 'extent of fair representation' nor even the cultural balance of that selection of knowledge, let alone the process by which it has been distilled from past and contemporary cultural capital. Far from it. Nor am I seeking to imply that it represents a fixed point around which all innovations must articulate and to which all other cultures must respond in a unilinear stimulus-response way.

Not at all. But on the other hand traditional British culture does represent a contemporary fact of life without which it would be unrealistic to reckon. And perhaps by showing the cultural distance between it and various cultural groups in our society, we can indicate how very much it needs to change, why and in which directions.

It will be helpful if the reader can imagine a cultural continuum between total separation and total absorption of cultural groups in society. Along this continuum will be located all cultural groups in terms of their relationship to each other and the overall cultural commonalities of any society, that is, those things which they have in common and which bind them together into what I have called a territorially defined political unit, a society. In some cases these commonalities will be weaker than in others. In some they will include language, religion, fundamental political and ethical beliefs and practices, such as democracy and the rule of law, and shared institutions, such as legal, political, social and economic, organizational 'edifices'.

Later in this book, when I am proposing a design for a multicultural curriculum, we shall have to agree on what those commonalities are for the United Kingdom. For the moment I think we can agree both that such commonalities exist and that they may be different in different societies. In some countries it would not include a common language, in others it would not involve a commitment to democratic process; in some, it would exclude the rule of law or include a different rule of law. But the subject of our deliberations here is society in the United Kingdom and it is its commonalities and the distance from these that we need to consider. Which returns me nicely to the idea of assimilation as a concept expressing relative distance from these commonalities.

Gordon, writing within a North American cultural context, has suggested seven what he calls 'subprocesses' in the overall process of assimilation! These, slightly altered for our purposes here, range from acculturation into the behavioural patterns of the society, through large-scale entrance into primary groups, large-scale intermarriage, the development of a sense of peoplehood with the society, absence of prejudice by that society, absence of discrimination by that society, to the absence of value and power conflict between groups, which really represents total absorption. Others have seen the process differently, envisaging both psychological and social dimensions and different stages.[2]

But Gordon's conceptualization is sufficient to my argument at the moment for it illustrates the fact that some social groups, and pupils in your school, will stand in a different relationship to your culture and that which you represent in your school than will others. The presuppositions on the basis of which you act will therefore be very different from those which apply if you had been working within a monist, that is, homogeneous society and educational system. (There you might just be able to argue that you should treat all pupils exactly alike). And so we come to one of the teacher's major dilemmas in a multi-cultural society, namely, whether he should ignore this cultural diversity and try to treat all children as the same in a multiracial society (should he act colour-blind for example?); or should he, on the other hand, seek to know more of the diversity which 'confronts' him and to take it into account in his teaching content and teaching strategies?

In my view, the teacher in a multicultural society, committed to equality of educational opportunity, must seek to engage that cultural diversity in 'creative dialogue'. Paradoxically, to do otherwise is automatically but inadvertently to discriminate and to deny equality of opportunity. For those who may stand in a weaker relationship to the commonalities, for instance, to language, will thereby be discriminated against and will thus have their disadvantage compounded. But the school will suffer too, because the absence of dialogue will just as surely impoverish the curriculum, personnel and structure of the school.

So the teacher walks a narrow line between ignoring and discriminating against, on the one side, and uncritical stereotyping based on 'half-knowledge', on the other. But the absence of simplistic 'do's' and 'don'ts', of easy tips, does not mean that there are no 'pegging points' to guide the teacher in making justifiable decisions, subject to publicly available criteria. Nor, as we shall see in the latter part of this chapter, is there an absence of admonitions, precepts and exemplars of how to walk that line and remain an 'upright' member of the teaching profession fully engaged for a multicultural society.

For the moment let us leave these precepts and exemplars on one side and suggest that the teacher needs to be aware of cultural diversity in his pupils and the surrounding community, to have positive attitudes towards its potential in his teaching, to be willing to engage in creative dialogue with his pupils and the surrounding community about the inclusion of their culture in his teaching, to manifest an active engagement against cultural prejudice and discrimination, and to possess the momentum to keep on 'interlearning' with his pupils and community throughout his professional life. Put briefly, educational action in the multicultural society implies dialogue, knowledge, awareness and positive predispositions towards cultural pluralism, and includes an alertness to the dangers of stereotyping, bias by omission (and in teaching materials) and the need for an understanding of the concept and practice of multiple social and occupational role occupancy. Above all it means accepting that different pupils will stand in different relationships not only to the teacher and culture of the school, but also to the content and teaching methods which the teacher deploys, and it means trying to act accordingly.

Creating an open classroom

We have all too few descriptions of the 'enactment'[3] of multicultural curricula in multi-cultural contexts – as opposed to prescriptive tallies of curriculum content – but one which brought home to me very graphically this point about cultural distance is the description by Jeffcoate of his observations of a downtown school serving an area of 'new council housing and flats and condemned and derelict streets', and with a 40 per cent representation of ethnic minority groups amongst its pupil body[4].

In his account of one multiracial classroom, Jeffcoate points to the way in which the teacher's questioning techniques gave an opportunity for the children to compare the content of the curriculum with their own knowledge and experience. To use his words, 'talking about slavery moved into talking about prejudice and discrimination today'.[5] As Jeffcoate points out, there were few taboo areas, and issues concerning such matters as sex, intermarriage and mixed race children could be tackled within the overall racial amity of the ethos of the class. You may read for yourself the fascinating accounts which Jeffcoate gives of his multiracial classroom, but the major message which emerges is of the need for teachers not only to be open, but to carry conviction with their pupils that they are sufficiently open for the pupils to say and write what they genuinely feel, and for teachers themselves to be critically aware of what their curriculum has achieved, to bring them closer to being what Bruner has called 'brothers in inquiry' with their pupils[6].

In July 1981, the Multiethnic Inspectorate of the Inner London Education Authority provided a 'first-base' *aide memoire* which tackles the questions of what kind of school ethos and atmosphere and which classroom strategies may assist in this process[7]. After a series of 'aspects for review' in which the question is posed as to whether teachers are aware of the role they play in creating an atmosphere and utilizing teaching methods which encourage pupils from different cultural groups to work together, the document indicates positive action which teachers may take to achieve such goals. To summarize, teachers are encouraged to:

a. create opportunities for social relationships to be extended across cultural and ethnic groups by:
   1. encouraging collaborative, small group work; and
   2. creating purposeful tasks, the solution to which can only be

achieved by working together;
b. develop an ethos which encourages pupils *(and teachers):*
   1. to question their own views of racial and cultural groups critically;
   2. be aware of the negative effects of negative views;
c. identify barriers to full participation in lessons by all pupils, for example, religious practices etc.

I have slightly paraphrased the goals but, I hope, without doing violence to their major thrust, which is the achievement of the open and tolerant classroom (and school) which Jeffcoate was describing.

The dangers of the 'hidden curriculum'

But in addition to providing a basis for conscious action on the part of the teacher, are there any difficulties which knowledge and professional commitment could innocently bring? Clearly the danger of stereotyping is always there and increased knowledge may increase the tendency.

The danger of seeking easy 'solutions' and simple explanatory generalizations is ever present. Does the evidence, for example, highlighted by Monica Taylor, of a strong trend to underachievement on the part of pupils of West Indian origin mean that teachers' expectations for the wide range of backgrounds and cultures which that description encompasses, should be appropriately low?[8] Clearly, if we want to avoid self-fulfilling prophecies, they should not, and in any case evidence of the achievement of West Indian migrants to the United States points in the opposite direction: they have higher levels of achievement than blacks who have been in the United States for many generations?

Teachers, too, may have quite unintentionally picked up negative stereotypes. They may see all pupils of West Indian origin as, for instance, disruptive or problem pupils. They may have absorbed conventional 'wisdoms' about Asians from society at large, the media or even their own books, materials and resources. Through these subconsciously absorbed 'wisdoms', they may unconsciously influence the development of self-concept in children from different ethnic origins and their social interaction and school achievement.

Bias in books and materials

Teachers must take particular note of the subliminal bias and racism of the materials which they use and attempt to redress the balance, bearing in mind that textbooks reflect the social climate in which they are written: its prejudices and discriminations. Whilst the research and writing in this field in the United Kingdom has been spasmodic and uncoordinated and much of the best work has come from North America and Australia,[10] more recent endeavours of individuals such as Hicks and of organizations such as The National Association for Multiracial Education, the Children's Rights Workshop, The National Committee on Racism in Children's Books, The Schools Council and the National Union of Teachers, have sought to fill the gap, by researching, writing and, in particular, providing helpful checklists against which teachers can 'measure' the multiculturalism of their books and materials. The most comprehensive set of such criteria or guidelines is probably that produced by the World Council of Churches Workshop on Racism in Children's and School Textbooks![11]

In the United States, however, individual Public School Boards have often generated their own general criteria for evaluating textual materials and the Ethnic Heritage Studies Program working at Federal level drew up a series of very detailed criteria for projects developing materials, under the following headings:

Criteria for technical quality – Print

Criteria for technical quality – Non-Print

Criteria for ethnic authenticity

Criteria for appropriateness for use in particular learning situations

Criteria for use as teacher resource materials

Criteria for use as student learning materials

Each of these main criteria was then further calibrated into subcriteria with further subdivisions as necessary![12]

Particular points which all guidelines share and of which all teachers should be aware are:

1. The need for the presence of members of ethnic minority groups in materials in a variety of roles on a more than token basis;
2. The incidence of stereotyping and its role in generating and reinforcing prejudice;
3. The occurrence of 'imperial past'-induced racism purporting to be conventional wisdom;
4. The use of language or particular style or vocabulary in a subliminally discriminating way;
5. The need for the treatment of controverisal issues in an 'open' way;
6. The tendency to caricature in illustrations or bias in the presentation of statistics and tables;
7. The need to regard textbooks, which age rapidly, as one source of evidence, to be jointly and critically appraised against contemporary society and its needs.

Teachers can help to improve pupils' intercultural attitudes

In this respect, research into the effects of teachers' racial attitudes on pupils' image of themselves, based on the recording and analysis of classroom interaction in 70 multiethnic classrooms, also gives us some insight into the case for teachers to look more deeply into their activities in the classroom (and how they may improve them) and to consider the impact of these activities, conscious and subconscious, on children's learning.[13] The results of research and writing from both the United Kingdom and the United States seem to confirm that teachers can have an effect on intercultural attitudes.

Stenhouse, for instance, summarizing the findings of a major project studying the effects of teaching on interracial attitudes, pulls them together in a series of hypotheses which bid fair to be an informal common-sense theory. Both 'committed' and 'neutral' teaching were found to be equally and moderately effective in combating racial prejudice, but the results were subject to the long-term need for reinforcement. The school or social context is not likely to achieve this unless there are specific and actively designed policies and practices for the school, addressed to this effect. One very interesting aspect of Stenhouse's remarkably lucid and frank account is the hypothesis that, where there is 'appeal to the educational judgement of those taught', this will lead to some children moving in the opposite direction to that desired. It seems apparent, that where teachers are engaged in teaching and not coercion or indoctrination, they must accept that some children may regress. But then that has always been an important distinction between education, where the clients are free, and brainwashing, where they are not![14]

Similarly in the United States, Banks, surveying and summarizing the findings of research into changing children's racial attitudes, after first emphasizing that any theory of prejudice must include a multi-dimensional explanation, comprehending personality variables, the power structure of society itself and the way it enculturates, and the social structure of institutions, lists a series of points which are worth referring to here. These include the fact that children's racial attitudes can be modified by objectives and strategies specifically designed for that purpose, but that specific instructional goals need to be clearly formulated and clearly defined teaching strategies need to be structured to that purpose. In other words, programmes should not consist of 'one-shot' treatments because incidental teaching is not usually effective. Banks also makes the point that systematic experiences need to be structured to reinforce and perpetuate desired attitudes and that visual materials greatly enhance effectiveness, particularly where material is used to present ethnic minority groups in a favourable light. He agrees that the prevalent attitude towards different races and groups in the social situation (institution) is a significant determinant of children's racial feelings, and that the attitudes and predispositions of the classroom teacher are important variables. Finally, he suggests that pupils who think at a high level and critically are less likely to show prejudice than pupils who reason at lower levels and think less critically[15]

In other words, the materials, teaching strategies, attitudes of the teacher, ethos of the school and atmosphere of the classroom all count, and open classrooms which continuously encourage pupils to participate on their own cultural terms and bring their own culture into play are more likely to achieve the purposes of multicultural education for a majority of the children.

The important thing to remember is that a stereotype is a cultural construct and teachers do have the power to suggest and propose alternative healthier constructs in line with the major principles of our society. This should, of course, be grounded in the understanding that categorizing and generalizing are natural functions of human thinking but also that the power structure of our society may itself be discriminatory. All the more reason then for pupils to learn to view each person as an individual, to respect his or her beliefs, to see him or her as an occupant of multiple social roles, and to question, most critically, generalizations about race and ethnic, sex and cultural background.

One way to tackle this is by role reversal: another by small group work exploring colour and colour association; another still by using several newspaper cuttings of the same incident (it might be what the *Daily Telegraph* and *The Guardian* used as their headlines on the publication of the Rampton Report) but tackled it must be. Failure to see this and to act upon it is as surely social irresponsibility as is the action of the media in deliberately beaming harmful stereotypes at young people. Of course, we have to remember that stereotypes are not just the result of attitudes but are also a part of 'social and cultural relations and structural inequalities'[16] but these latter are not inevitable and unchanging. They are subject to the deliberate influence of human will: and that means that teachers do have an influence and can work to counteract racism. The alternative to such a position is that teachers have no influence and schools do not matter except to endorse what is already there: a deterministic and pessimistic philosophy of life indeed.

Bias by omission

Just as surely, however, as teachers can influence for change and healthy racial attitudes, they can by omission, silence or lack of prudence endorse the very stereotypes which at an overt level they are committed to fighting. As a teacher who attended a workshop on multicultural education where I was giving a talk put it, 'in a school where there are only one or two *of them*, isn't it better not to draw attention to differences?'. and later 'After all, the days of Empire and slavery are past, isn't it better to concentrate on what unites us?'[17]

The question tends to present a false choice of alternatives: ignore the differences (and presumably inequalities, prejudice and discrimination) and no one will notice them. Concentrate on the similarities and all will be well. My response to this is that surely we have to emphasize what unites us and what we have in common and this view will have emerged for the reader from my first chapter. But this cannot be to the exclusion, or indeed the suppression of an understanding, awareness and sensitive affirmation of legitimate difference. Indeed, somewhat paradoxical though it may seem, this latter quality should be something which we have in common. Thus, it should be obvious (though apparently it is not) that an active engagement for racial and cultural difference is an essential part of any multicultural education strategy.

Naturally, the teacher will need to exercise enormous sensitivity and circumspection, but it is not just (as implied in the quotation) in schools where ethnic minority students are small in numbers, where pupils may be uncomfortable with their 'ethnic identity', but also in schools with large numbers. For, as Banks points out, pupils can sense when there is intolerance, prejudice and discrimination towards their own ethnic group. They do not need to be told explicitly, and indeed many of the 'cues' can be 'non-verbal' ones![18] But the message is the same.

Now I am not arguing that pupils should be forced to discuss their own ethnic or cultural characteristics. Nor do I suggest that pupils should be put in a position where they have to identify or not with an ethnic group. On the contrary, all pupils – and all members of a multicultural society – have the right to choose, and it is in this sense that multicultural education must aim to be truly emancipatory. But faced with the apparent dilemma of respecting the individual right of pupils to choose and the need to discuss fundamental issues of cultural difference in our society, what can the teacher do?

This is a complex and difficult question and one which defies simplistic 'rule of thumb' answers. Early and admittedly very limited research in England seemed to indicate that teaching to undermine prejudice might have the opposite effect[19] although research quoted above from the United Kingdom and the United States contradicts this. I am sensitive to Stuart Hall's admonition that people have strong emotional ideological positions about race but this strong emotional charge has to be recognized and brought out.[20] I am conscious, too, of the point which I quoted earlier from Banks's survey of research, that prejudice, discrimination and stereotyping are functions not only of personality, but of societal and institutional structure and power distribution.

For all these reasons, difficult issues of cultural differences, prejudice, stereotyping, discrimination and race have to be part of an overall, holistic strategy of multicultural education in the school and in the classroom. Unless they are, the time-bomb of hidden prejudice will eventually explode if untackled or explode if handled insensitively. The issues cannot be omitted, for to omit is to consent and reinforce.

Thus the issue is not whether to include the issues surrounding cultural diversity in the curriculum or not, but rather *how* to include them so that they may arise naturally in a classroom atmosphere where the pupils know that acceptance and respect for ethnic differences are grounded in an appreciation of commonality, and where they (the pupils) are used to the expectation that they make reflective decisions concerning their own values, opinions and actions, and as a means of resolution of personal and social problems. (Naturally, I am not suggesting that humans, either adults or children, can ever be totally analytic and non-emotional).

The gimmicky, folksy tokenism of so much of the early attempts at multiculturalism in the United Kingdom was ineffective and even counterproductive. Not only did such attempts tend to neglect the cogent influence of the social structure of institutions on prejudice but even within the individual classroom they concentrated on ad hoc, randomly selected items (often of cultural difference), focused on fairly low levels of cognitive functioning. Such 'ritual-like' activities could even do harm, for they may, by their spasmodic, ad hoc and piecemeal introduction and low level of intellectual demand on the pupils, reinforce the idea that ethnic minority cultures are exotic, different and not really a full part of British society. What I am arguing they should do, is to take the issue holistically and in terms of teaching strategies and content, and aim at high levels of cognitive sophistication, encouraging clear thinking, critical reasoning, the posing of probing questions, concept attainment, analysis, decision-making and social action.[21]

So, to summarize briefly the argument in this chapter so far:

1. Cultural diversity is both opportunity and challenge; omission of discussion of cultural diversity is bias.
2. The teacher has a positive responsibility to introduce discussion of cultural diversity (including issues of racial prejudice) sensitively and as part of an overall, 'long-lasting' strategy of multicultural education.
3. Pupils have the same rights to privacy and choice of ethnic identity as all members of a multicultural society.
4. Classroom materials and texts need to be rigorously appraised for their bias in general and racism in particular.
5. Only a classroom (and school) ethos and active policies, where the culture and practice are understood by all parties to be accepting and affirmative of cultural difference, will provide a seedbed for fruitful discussion of potentially explosive and emotional issues of race, cultural differences, etc.
6. There must be a 'tradition' of the expectation of reflective decision-making by pupils and teachers; one-off approaches may do more harm than good; long-term reinforcement is necessary.
7. Multicultural strategies and content must aim at a high level of cognitive functioning, including concept attainment, decision-making and affirmative engagement for social action.
8. Where the above educational strategies are implemented, teachers can expect to have a positive effect on children's inter-cultural attitudes, but some children may be expected to move in the undesired direction.

The work of Stenhouse and his colleagues

Agreed, the reader may say, but how? Even if I accept the ground-rules you are proposing, what I need is examples of how other people have tackled this problem, which you admit is very sensitive and where once again I am walking a tightrope with different people pushing me in different directions and others just waiting and hoping that I will fall off. Are there any examples of teaching which illustrate the principles you have summarized?

Once again we are faced with the paucity of good examples of the 'how' of multicultural education as opposed to the 'what'. But in this respect we are fortunate in having available the results of work carried out by Professor Lawrence Stenhouse and his colleagues at the University of East Anglia with teachers, schools, students and pupils. At the risk of doing injustice, through abridgement and possible distortion, to what is a complex developmental approach which has been constantly refined in response to criticism over a period of some 15 years, I am going to select three elements at this stage, which, I hope, will encourage those readers who are not already familiar with the work to look more closely at the whole output. The three elements I have selected are: the impartial chairman; the teacher as researcher; and the consideration of content as evidence for discussion.

The idea of the role of the teacher as procedurally impartial (or neutral) chairman is not only central to the Humanities Curriculum Project but also to the concept of an education which is emancipatory, fostering the judgement of children, rather than seeking to coerce their compliance. It is controversial and appears to have been one major element which led to the Humanities 'Race Pack' not being published[22] The background to this is Stenhouse's view of teaching as being the empowering of children, not the coercion of them. It is 'not merely instruction, but the systematic promotion of learning by whatever means'. The improvement of teaching is seen as being accessible by the thoughtful refinement of professional skill achieved by the gradual elimination of failings through the systematic study of one's own teaching[23] Content is seen not as answer, authority, solution, but as grist to the mill of the formulation of judgement.

The roles of the teacher as *impartial chairman* and as *researcher* are thus seen as complementary aspects of a pedagogy of emancipation which can generate a climate of openness, rather than one of closure, where the orientation is to teaching strategies rather than content, to the utilization of knowledge rather than assessment, to problems rather than ready-made solutions, to a climate of uncertainty, provisionality, value divergence and research, rather than prescription, certainty and a false consensus. As Stenhouse succinctly puts it, the teaching is through a 'loyalty to the spirit of inquiry'[24] rather than 'instruction through a rhetoric of conclusions'[25]

Combined with the results of research carried out at the University of East Anglia and the formulation of hypotheses, quoted above, what we have here are some tentative guiding principles for the achievement of an 'open classroom' for multicultural education, such as I argued previously is essential to enable pupils to engage in speculative discourse, in confident dialogue, in critical judgement, in sensitive and affirmative interlearning with their peers, and teachers, and such as will facilitate the discussion of the complex, difficult and critical human issues of our contemporary society. I have already made the point, of course, that what happens in the classroom is influenced by what happens outside, and that pupils treated to such adult fare in the classroom will have corresponding expectations outside in the corridors, in morning assembly and on the sportsfield. As the Schools Council Working Paper 2, put it:

> ... adult procedures in the classroom... will not be successful if a different kind of relationship between teacher and pupil obtains in the corridor or in extra-curricular activity. If the teacher emphasizes, in the classroom, his common humanity in the face of many problems, the pupils will not take kindly to being demoted to the status of children in other relationships within the same institution. Indeed, they may write off the classroom relationship as a 'soft-sell'.[26]

In other words, what happens in the classroom in terms of the building of a better ethos for dialogue and appreciation of a common humanity has to be backed up by a congruent approach to these matters in all that the school does. But I shall return to this issue in Chapters Three and Four. For the moment I will revert to the classroom level.

Some classroom approaches

We have, from the Centre for Applied Research in Education at the University of East Anglia, a comprehensive introduction to the problems and techniques of discussion teaching which has been compiled by Humanities Curriculum Project (HCP) teachers and edited by Jean Rudduck.[27] Whilst leaving open the availability of other approaches to discussion, and indeed encouraging teachers to consider alternatives to the approach to discussion presented in the document, this publication presents a useful series of topics surrounding the issue of discussion as a method of teaching. It looks, for example, at why both pupils and students find discussion difficult. It appraises the role of the teacher in discussion and describes a number of roles open to him/her, including the instructor, the participant, the devil's advocate, the neutral chairman, and the consultant. It looks at the discussion of issues and considers a number of strategies whereby issues may be raised, even venturing a definition of what a controversial issue is. It considers the use of evidence in discussion, and the nature of evidence, citing the aim of discussion as being understanding, and considering the nature of that understanding. Analysing discussion, it proposes criteria for such analysis and suggests questions which may be asked by the teacher, hypotheses, ground rules and criteria for identifying progress. Finally, an attempt is made to assist the teacher in observing behaviour in the discussion group by means of a chart which identifies some common problems in discussion work and which offers evidence to help teachers to recognize the problems.

The reader is encouraged to set each and every one of the units in the book against a practical situation, and transcripts and tapes are provided in order to relate this relationship to practice. Teachers are encouraged to use the publication as a basis for training and commentaries are given on sequences from the transcripts. For example, in the section on roles open to the teacher in discussion an instance is given of an attempt by a teacher to fulfil the role of neutral chairman where she is not apparently committed to that role and does not, in fact, succeed in it. The transcript is annotated in order to indicate the way in which the teacher subsequently moves from an 'instructor' strategy onto one of 'devil's advocate' and subsequently into the instructor strategy once again before adopting the role of a dominant participant. Suggestions are then made at the end, of the way in which teachers might find it useful to monitor the extent to which they move in and out of roles in discussion in the classroom, and what effects these roles have or appear to have on pupil responses.[28] The emphasis is on the ways and extent to which the teacher can improve teaching by a systematic study of his/her performance. I must say that the idea of being able to 'triangulate' my own impressions with those of others, including pupils, is one which both challenges and 'calls to discourse'. It is, it seems to me, one useful means whereby the kind of more open classroom we have been seeking to construct can be achieved.

A further publication which gives some insight into the practical classroom application of teaching strategies concerned with controversial issues, from the National Association for Race Relations Teaching and Action Research,[29] gives an account of an attempt to assess three strategies for teaching about race relations. One of these is the Humanities Project technique where the teacher adopts the role of a neutral chairman of a discussion group and where printed material, which is envisaged as evidence, is made available to the discussion group at appropriate points and subjected to critical appraisal. A second strategy based on improvised drama took place in schools where drama teaching was an already well established part of the curriculum, and a third which was not based on any existing and well-defined approach, within the 16 schools which participated.

Each of the groups of teachers adopting the three kinds of strategies had slightly differing aims, thus for example whilst the first group intended 'to develop an understanding, in the area of race relations, of social situations and human acts and of the value issues which they raise', the common purpose arrived at in the case of the second strategy was 'to educate for the elimination of racial tensions and ill-feeling within our society which is, and will be, multi-racial, by undermining prejudice, by developing respect for various traditions and by encouraging mutual understanding, reasonableness and justice'. In the case of the third strategy the aim of the teachers was 'to examine and illuminate those factors which relate directly to relationships in multi-ethnic groups'.[30]

Almost a thousand hours of classroom recordings were collected, and discussions of pupils assessing the work without a teacher present were also recorded. Additionally, written comments were provided by teachers who were also interviewed by members of the central research team. Thus, the team was in a position, not only to hear what occurred in each classroom, but also to collect information concerning the views of teachers and pupils about what went on. The resulting transcripts are illustrative of a range of classroom situations and experiences which, whilst making no claim to be fully comprehensive, are nonetheless illustrative of certain common areas of experience around three major themes: group relationships in the classroom, teaching about race relations, and the effects of teaching about race relations. These three main areas are then divided into further sub-headings which often take the form of a question that a teacher might ask about teaching about race relations. Such questions include issues of inter-ethnic attitudes within groups, the position of isolated minority group members and the tendency for white pupils to dissociate their black friends from blacks in general. Interestingly, in the context of the misgivings expressed earlier in this chapter concerning the effects of teaching about controversial issues, in the section on the effects of teaching about race relations, common doubts about the efficacy of teaching about race relations are touched on, including whether it can have negative results.[31]

In these two instances we have access to information about alternative approaches to the 'how' of multicultural education, or at least to one aspect of it, namely race relations, for I do not wish to give the impression that I consider race relations to be the whole of the multicultural curriculum. Moreover, we have not only transcripts but also tape recordings with accompanying commentary and archival back-up in the form of indexes of issues raised and subjective appraisals of the effectiveness of particular strategies. Neither of these two sets of material would claim to provide a comprehensive panacea in terms of teaching strategies which can be adopted in teaching about controversial issues. On the other hand, both of them give examples of how other teachers have attempted to tackle the same or similar problems. Neither of them would oppose the commonly heard argument that all classrooms are unique, but then surely this does not mean that we cannot learn from the strengths and weaknesses of the ways in which others have attempted to tackle similar problems?

Some alternative approaches

A more directive approach to educational strategies for teaching ethnic awareness, albeit one aimed predominantly at the elementary school, is contained in the work of Edith King. Here specific activities for the multiethnic elementary school are given. A series of activities is presented, including activities designed to promote ethnic awareness and self-identity amongst children, activities aimed at developing an ethnic chart story or teaching about ethnicity with pupils, or a multiethnic dolls-house project. Whilst the language is, on occasions, slightly 'off-putting', each activity contains an introduction giving an overall description of the strategy, detailed objectives, materials, procedures, follow-up activities and annotated bibliographies, including reference to appropriate resources.[32]

Similarly the work of Gloria Grant is worth referring to briefly in this connection. For her material includes 51 activities covering such curriculum areas as social studies, language, science, mathematics and art. A format is utilized in order to categorize the activities across concepts such as rationale, experiences, suggestions, evaluation notes and supplementary activities and the material includes ideas, methods and procedures which may help teachers to achieve multicultural learning goals for pupils. The interesting aspect of this material is the way in which it adopts the sort of overriding and holistic approach to multicultural education I have argued for in this chapter, involving the cultural and individual differences of all persons, regardless of their racial, ethnic, cultural, religious backgrounds or physical differences.[33]

Similarly, endorsing the need to aim at high levels of functioning, the work of Garcia presents a critical thinking exercise and activity to stimulate thought about issues in multicultural education, including self-analysis exercises, human rights exercises, communal theory exercises and self-study activities which can be used as springboards to in-depth analysis and assessment of value issues pertinent to multicultural education.[34]

For those teachers who are interested in language across the curriculum, and a more formal approach, Hansen-Krening provides suggestions for activities and appraisal across such areas as music and listening, art and the art of speaking, teaching basic writing skills through realistic fiction, movement and non-verbal communication, creative drama, including myths, legends, and folk tales, and in some cases model lessons presented in a structured format. Clearly this is not everyone's cup of tea but it does go some way towards assisting us with responses to the eternal question, 'How do I set about it? If only I could see examples of what other people have done I could then learn from it'.[35]

Clearly, these represent only a few examples from the vast range of material available within the United Kingdom or produced in other countries such as the United States, Australia and Canada, which can enable us to look at what multicultural education might mean for the teacher (in particular, how it can be implemented in the classroom) and to provide examples which may appeal to the diversity of persons, personalities and potentials in the teaching profession. I have been careful to emphasize that the one or two examples which I have been able to give do not represent any final decision with regard to the implementation of multicultural education but rather illustrate one or two aspects of the guiding principles I proposed. There are many roads to implementation and, in the last resort, these will be dependent on the individual classroom, the individual teacher and the group of pupils with whom he has to do. It will thus be clear to the reader that whereas the why's of multicultural education may be obtainable on a basis of broad consensus (yet to be achieved), this cannot be the case with regard to the how, what and where of its implementation, so that the answer to the question posed at the beginning of this chapter, 'What does multicultural education mean for me?', must ultimately be a personal one negotiated between the teacher and the learners involved and between them and their wider community.

Strategies for multicultural education

But this brings me to the second question which I posed at the beginning of this chapter, namely, 'Are there any examples of multicultural curricula' (of the 'what' of multicultural education) from which I can learn? Here there have been a number of 'macro-conceptualizations', or broad categorizations, of the array of different approaches to multicultural education and to the multicultural curriculum in particular, of which I shall refer to three: one by Gibson, one by Williams, and one by Lynch. I will conclude the chapter by making reference to half a dozen specific examples of multicultural curricula, which have been proposed in a number of different countries.

First, however, it is necessary to understand the genesis of multicultural education in order to comprehend the confusion which still surrounds the term. In all countries the commitment to multicultural education has arisen initially within the context of a disadvantage or deficit approach to educational provision and understanding of cultural capital. In many cases newly arrived immigrant groups—in the United States, in some cases, longer established cultural groups such as the blacks—have felt excluded from mainstream culture and equal access to educational opportunity within an allegedly democratic society where equality of opportunity is promised. In some cases, this has produced a so-called compensatory approach which has been brought about by social unrest and even riot: compelling knee-jerk reflexes from recalcitrant governments in the form of special provision for particular ethnic groups. The Black Studies and Ethnic Heritage Programs in the United States are a good example of this, as are analogue developments in Canada and Australia. Only gradually has a more holistic view of multicultural education, as an integral part of strategies for equality of educational opportunity, emerged in each of these countries, addressed to the population as a whole, and seeing education as a whole.

A categorization of different approaches (Gibson)
This aetiology is reflected in the conceptualization by Gibson of different educational strategies or approaches to multicultural education.[36] Systematizing the alternative approaches to conceptualizing multicultural education, based on a review of the educational literature in the United States, Gibson distinguishes five approaches, examining them in terms of differing objectives, the conditions which gave rise to the approach, its major proponents, the underlying assumptions regarding values, strategies, outcomes and target populations.

The five approaches are:
1. Education of the culturally different, or benevolent multiculturalism.
2. Education about educational differences, or cultural understanding.
3. Education for cultural pluralism.
4. Bicultural education.
5. Multicultural education as the norm for all pupils.

The first of these, education for the culturally different, is seen as being a mainstream dominated, compensatory, special programme which allegedly aims at equalizing educational opportunity by addressing the needs solely of children from certain ethnic minority groups. The culture of ethnic minorities is seen as 'in deficit' and therefore more capital has to be banked in order to put them in 'credit', so to speak.

The second strategy, education about cultural difference or cultural understanding, arises from demands from ethnic groups that schools should become more sensitive to cultural difference and modify their curricula accordingly. It aims to teach children to value cultural difference. Although it is said to be aimed at all children, its focus on difference may be seen as subtly leading to a reinforcement of conflict and of inferiority/superiority syndromes.

The third strategy, education for cultural pluralism, arises from the rejection of ethnic minority groups of a majority-enforced melting-pot approach to education, and it seeks to preserve, foster and extend cultural pluralism. It is, if you like, a minority group programme for the majority and as such it may be seen as creating, or at least preserving, boundaries between groups.

Bicultural education, the fourth strategy, is again only a partial approach which arises from the wish on the part of certain ethnic minority communities to maintain their own culture, but again it is predominantly addressed to minority students and indeed tends to be focused predominantly on language.

In the case of the final strategy, multicultural education, seen as the normal human experience of a multicultural society, an attempt is made to develop a comprehensive strategy of multicultural education addressed to all pupils and grounded in the ethos and needs of the multicultural society. The last strategy regards multicultural education as a process whereby individuals develop competencies in multiple cultural systems utilized to generate standards for perceiving, evaluating, believing and doing. It seeks to incorporate the previous four approaches. This latter strategy has, of course, its own inherent weaknesses, not least the diffusion of the concepts involved, the danger of a take-over and dominance by mainstream culture, and its relatively immature stage of development and, therefore, lack of examples.

The work of Gibson gives us an opportunity to learn from the experience and academic endeavour of others. It clearly identifies the dangers in partial strategies if they are unrelated to an overall concept of where society is going and what kind of curriculum it is attempting to pursue, seen as a whole. This is not to argue that any of the first four strategies is either unnecessary or unworthy but merely that it is insufficient on its own to the demands of a multicultural society for multicultural education. Indeed the advantage of the conceptualization, I would suggest, is the overview which it gives of both strategies addressed to special needs and those addressed to the needs of all.

A categorization of different curricula (Williams)

The work of Williams offers a different and slightly less sophisticated approach to a categorization of perspectives on the multicultural curriculum.[37] After identifying the gap between the experts and the majority of practitioners in the field, she attempts to clarify different approaches which she argues arise from different definitions of problems, themselves deriving in turn from different ideological perspectives. These latter, she suggests, lead to differing policy recommendations and curriculum and teaching outcomes.

The three perspectives of the multicultural curriculum which she identifies are labelled as the technicist approach, the moral approach and the socio-political approach. Each of these perspectives is considered against a paradigm including the central value assumptions, the educational ideology, the problem to be remedied, the type of programmes recommended and the curriculum emphasis.

The technicist approach is said to rest upon the assumption that the main problems and solutions within education relate to the development of educational skills and are best solved by the experts within the teaching profession. It is a compensatory educational ideology which accepts the need for special provision for members of ethnic minority groups and emphasizes improvements in basic skills and a focus upon poor self-concept as the main cause of under-achievement.

The moral perspective is seen as having, as its central concern, action aimed at diminishing prejudice and discrimination. It addresses all pupils within a school and not just minority children; it seeks to remedy the problem of the banking concept of education and authoritarian relationships within the classroom. Its curricular emphases are on countering prejudice and discrimination and it focuses on a wide range of feelings and emotions as a basis for discussion.

A third strategy, a so-called sociopolitical one, is said to have as its central value assumption the concept of justice within a plural society. It sees knowledge as power and adopts a holistic approach to problems of identity and alienation in order to achieve the permeation of the whole curriculum with a multicultural emphasis and the provision of skills with which to fight for rights (and presumably access to power and resources in society).

It will be clear that there are certain conceptual similarities between the Gibson and Williams typologies and yet they derive from different cultural backgrounds and national intellectual styles. They both, for example, seek to identify the ideological precursors of particular strategies and to assess their strengths and weaknesses on the basis of literature search and conceptualization. Each seeks to clarify which section of the population is addressed, and whether a holistic approach, sensitive to issues of access to resources and power in society, is available. In both cases there is a dichotomy between strategies which are holistic and those which are partial, those which concern all pupils and those which concern only segments of the pupil population, whether majority or minority pupils. An attempt is also made to test the political consequences of the educational knowledge involved.

A categorization of different tactics

In contrast to the above categorizations, the one developed by the author on the basis of an empirical study of multicultural teacher education in Australia looks mainly at what I shall call curricular tactics.[38] It is concerned, in particular, with appraising the strategies of how to introduce multicultural education into teacher education curricula. The conceptual framework developed, is given below with examples adapted to the British context.

Parallel Under this tactic whole course provision is attempted at the side of other (non-multicultural) curricula. For instance, units in multicultural education, immigrant education, Black Studies, Asian Studies, Caribbean Studies, the teaching of English as a foreign language, are already built up as *immigrant* groups settle in an area and, realizing their exclusion from the common culture and the exclusion of their culture from the curriculum, begin to make special demands to balance this. As the Report of the Parliamentary Select Committee in 1982 pointed out, 'A Black Studies Curriculum can become an educational ghetto for black pupils.'[39] It is often multidisciplinary, sometimes involving mere knowledge, sometimes also including affective dispositions, but the injection into the curriculum is at a non-prestigious part and level of the provision. It may include mother-tongue instruction but is more often based on an ideology of deficit and, as in the United States, mother-tongue instruction is seen by and large as an interim measure to full monolingual competence. On the other hand, there is strong emphasis on the demand for one such tactic, namely mother-tongue *maintenance* and a general support for the need for it in schools.[40]

Additive This involves small units, modules or components added to existing curricula in order to achieve additional knowledge or perspectives, for example, in Art, History, Religion etc. There is minimal dislocation to existing hierarchies of knowledge. Trendy nonsense and 'folksy tokenism' abound, used like baubles on a Christmas tree, but on the other hand, it often represents a first step or point of entry to a more radical reappraisal. In that sense, it can be seen as a transition stage.

Permeation   This involves the internal rearticulation or redesign *ab initio* of the epistemology or knowledge structure of existing courses. New structures of knowledge are seen to imply a complete reform of the whole curriculum, including changes in values, the structure of knowledge and the institutional context too. Over-radical and threatening for some, one of its major problems is a lack of appropriate expertise, for it demands very confident and very sophisticated teachers. It sometimes includes internal organization and community links. On the other hand, the Little-Willey Report indicated that 68 per cent of school staff had discussed this approach and 94 per cent of teachers in schools with a concentration of 30 per cent or more of ethnic minority pupils.[41] The Schools Council Project Report *Education for a Multiracial Society (5-13)* has dimensions committed to this approach.[42]

Materials Production Approach   This can aim at either of the above tactics ranging from a predominantly technical, knowledge-based approach to the broader and more affective purposes and strategies of, for instance, the Race Pack and the Humanities Curriculum Project at the national level. It may include material produced at a district level, for example, Bradford Metropolitan District[43] and materials produced at school level too, for example, Birley High School.[44] It is often a very useful method of focusing attention and a means of cooperative endeavour and 'getting started'. In its more sophisticated form, the material is used in the development of open classroom discussion, the teacher becoming a researcher.

Consultancy Approach This tactic is normally institutionally cooperative in the sense that a dialogical approach is adopted with local advisers, syndicates, teacher education tutors, etc. Sometimes institutions strive together to help each other. It may involve links between multiracial and non-multiracial schools, links with the Council for Racial Equality, or with university and polytechnic Departments of Education, and with overseas institutions. In this sense it often 'brims over' into global or development education. Sometimes teachers are sent abroad, for example to the Indian sub-continent or Caribbean to gain experience.

Research/Action Research There are an increasing number of projects, although still far too few, which adopt a pure policy-oriented or action research approach. The Bedford and Bradford language projects are good examples of an action-research approach and the work of Little and Willey, Verma and Bagley, Verity Khan, John Rex and the Aston Unit represent different degrees of 'power' sensitivity and policy orientation, ranging through institutional, systemic and societal levels.

Designs for multicultural curricula

I may have given the impression in the preceding section that I consider the 'what' of the curriculum to be unimportant compared to the 'how'. I must now restore the balance by making it quite clear that in order for any curriculum to be implemented the 'what' and the 'how' are both indispensable and indeed that in practice they are usually symbiotic. For this reason, having considered a number of examples of the 'how' of multicultural curriculum development, this chapter concludes with a number of examples of the 'what' drawn from different countries. In introducing them, it is as well to emphasize that a major thrust of this book is towards the idea that there is a 'limited distinct body of knowledge worth transmitting to the entire younger generation'.[45] But that additional richness must be available, and based on personal, cultural, social, vocational and environmental needs.

First, however, a number of preliminary points must be made. For instance, whilst the development of a multicultural curriculum for all children is no doubt a very radical departure from what has been achieved so far in the vast majority of schools, it is clear from the conceptualizations of multicultural curricula which have been given thus far at the macro level, that it can be tackled in a modest and unobtrusive way to begin with, and that many teachers have already begun to travel this road. There are many roads to the multicultural curriculum and it is far preferable to begin in an unspectacular way and move from that bridgehead into more radical reform, than to seek to attain it in one fell swoop and fail, damaging the prospects of the introduction of such a curriculum for a long time to come.

Secondly, whilst the Schools Council report is correct concerning the increasing difficulty of introducing a multicultural policy across the curriculum with the advancing age of the children, it is nonetheless also the case that a multicultural curriculum is a crucial, fundamental and core element of the learning of all children for as long as they are at school and that it should permeate all areas of their curriculum, though of course differentially, whatever the age level of the pupils concerned,[46] and the summaries of work by Stenhouse and Banks would appear to confirm the need for ongoing reinforcement if long term effects are desired.

Thirdly, I am conscious of the fact that to give the overall pattern of curriculum implementation is to jump the gun slightly, insofar as it leaves implicit the kinds of objectives which are to be attained. In each case therefore, whilst the main emphasis of the description is placed upon the content, reference is made to the source where more details of the aims can be found.

Fourthly, the reader will have gathered that I have mixed feelings about a model which includes the specification of behavioural objectives for a multicultural curriculum. Whilst I am careful not to rule it out completely, it can be argued that it leads to an assumption of a mechanistic relationship between objectives and the 'what' and 'how' of curriculum implementation, or conversely to the bypassing of any holistic concept of a multicultural curriculum, through the introduction of objectives into specific educational activities or themes or subject areas without any overall conceptual framework of the curriculum as a whole, let alone of its essential and irreducible core components.

A multicultural curriculum

That said, one of the most influential initiatives in the field of multicultural curriculum development has been that which was fostered and adopted by Jeffcoate, aiming at what he calls the idea of a multiracial curriculum. Emphasizing the distinction between transformationist and transmissionist education, Jeffcoate builds up on the basis of a classification of objectives, addressed predominantly to respect for others and respect for self, the idea of a curriculum which reflects the multiracialism of Britain and the world and draws significantly on the experiences of British racial minorities and cultures overseas.[47]

The foci of this curriculum, respect for others and respect for self, would each contain both cognitive knowledge and skills and affective components including attitudes, values and emotional sets.[48]

Within the cognitive area important knowledge for all pupils would include the basic facts of race and racial difference; of customs, values and beliefs of the main cultures represented in Britain, and particularly the local community, and the reasons for the immigration of different groups to Britain, and to that local community. Parallel to this, cognitive knowledge under the heading of 'respect for self' would include the history and achievements of the pupil's own culture and what is distinctive about it. Under cognitive skills, pupils would be expected to be able to evaluate their own culture objectively and be aware of stereotyping and scapegoating from whatever source they come and whatever medium is used. Similarly emphasis is placed on efficient communication in English and in the mother-tongue if it is different from English. Affective objectives under both heads, amongst others, relate to an acceptance of the widespread nature of prejudice and discrimination, a positive self-image and confidence in their sense of their own identities.

A list of criteria for the selection of learning experiences is then defined which includes the opportunity for 'cultures from overseas' to be allowed to speak for themselves and the need for the curriculum to be both international in its content and global in its perspective.

A polyethnic survival curriculum

A very different model is offered by Bullivant. In his proposal for a polyethnic survival curriculum for pupils living in societies such as Australia and New Zealand, he suggests five core elements, none of which is an academic discipline in its own right and each of which derives its subject matter from a range of contributory subjects or disciplines.[49]

The five core elements are:
1. Communicative competence.
2. Political and economic education.
3. Numeracy.
4. Moral and social education.
5. Environmental awareness.

This is a very important contribution to the debate concerning the shape and content of a multicultural core curriculum, both because of the elements which are included and the meaning which is given to those elements. For example, under political and economic competence, Bullivant attempts to provide for the acquisition by pupils of knowledge and skills which they will need in order to understand and cope with the networks and structures which control access to the goods, resources and other rewards of a society. In this sense, Bullivant's definition of a multicultural curriculum is power-sensitive and realistic in a way which few other proposals for the development of multicultural curricula have been so far. Additionally, it also attempts a holistic definition of a multicultural core curriculum and seeks to provide an overall shape for such a curriculum. Bullivant's proposal is also important for the extensive way in which the area of political and economic competence is further exemplified and illustrated by the relationship to the modes of study involved and the identification of topics for particular stages of psychological development. Additionally, an outline syllabus for classes 1-6 is given with a summary of general aims and specific details of syllabuses including themes, topics and suggested modes of enquiry, together with an identification of the principles involved.[50]

Education courses for a multicultural society

Smolicz, writing similarly within an Australian context, seeks to prescribe what he terms 'educational courses for a multicultural society'.[51] Once again, as with the previous two examples, the proposals are addressed to all pupils. Smolicz makes it clear in defining the kinds of courses which he proposes that their introduction and continued success rests on the presupposition of the existence of a general multicultural orientation or perspective in all school programmes, practices, policies and in the ethos of the school. His proposals are also linked to the identification of a number of conditions for continued cultural pluralism within Australia. To these ends, he identifies particular school courses which will help to provide for conditions of pluralism and social cohesion.

The six kinds of courses are: multicultural education; ethnic education concerned with ethnic studies; ethnic education concerned with community languages; bilingual education; English as a second language; and education for bilingual/bicultural teachers and other educators. Each of these courses is then considered in terms of its aims, its general emphasis, the students for whom it is intended, and the educational level.[52]

The importance of this proposal is the differentiation which it introduces between the kinds of educational provision which are necessary for ongoing differentiation within society and the kind of common course which is indispensable, not only to a tolerance of that difference but also to continuing social cohesion.

A multiethnic curriculum

In the United States, the American writer Banks has conceptualized not only models of multi-ethnic education but also of ethnic studies. The example which follows however is drawn from his work on multiethnic education where he conceptualizes a series of model approaches ranging from a total Anglo-American perspective on history and culture, through multiethnic perspectives as additives to a major curriculum thrust, to a completely multiethnic curriculum in which every historical and social event is viewed from the perspectives of different ethnic groups. A further progression is represented by a fourth model – an ethnonational model – as the ultimate curriculum goal where students study historical and social

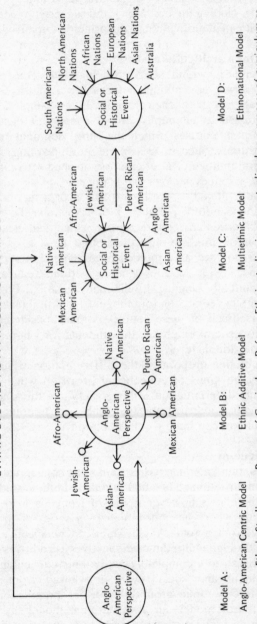

Figure 2

ETHNIC STUDIES AS A PROCESS OF CURRICULUM REFORM

Model A: Anglo-American Centric Model

Model B: Ethnic Additive Model

Model C: Multiethnic Model

Model D: Ethnonational Model

Ethnic Studies as a Process of Curriculum Reform. Ethnic studies is conceptualized as a process of curriculum reform which can lead from a total Anglo-American perspective on our history and culture (Model A), to multiethnic perspectives as additives to the major curriculum thrust (Model B), to a completely multiethnic curriculum in which every historical and social event is viewed from the perspectives of different ethnic groups (Model C). In Model C the Anglo-American perspective is only one of several and is in no way superior or inferior to other ethnic perspectives. Model D, which is multinational, is the ultimate curriculum goal. In this curriculum model, students study historical and social events from multinational perspectives and points of view. Many schools that have attempted ethnic modification of the curriculum have implemented Model B types of programs. It is suggested here that curriculum reform move directly from Model A to Model C and ultimately to Model D. However, in those districts which have Model B types of programs, it is suggested that they move from Model B to Model C and eventually to Model D types of curricular organizations.

events from multinational perspectives and points of view. (See Figure 2)[53]

A core multicultural curriculum

The next example of an attempt to build a curriculum which will be inherently multicultural is taken from the work of the Curriculum Development Centre in Australia. Emphasizing that the core curriculum which it is proposing comprises fundamental learnings for all students and not a definition of all learnings in the whole curriculum, the material focuses on the common culture, the common multiculture, common learnings, the contemporarily relevant aspects of education, the basic essential learnings, the structure of learnings, the common learning situations and common applied learning tasks[54]

After identifying some of the major common values of the Australian way of life it seeks to identify what it calls certain basic learning tools and resources, including such items as communicating in spoken and written language, number skills, scientific processes, etc., manual and physical skills, the management of bodily and mental health, the capacity to use and apply knowledge symbols, etc. It then proceeds to build a framework for a core curriculum including core learning processes such as learning and thinking techniques, ways of organizing knowledge, dispositions and values, etc., and core learning, comprising areas of knowledge and experience.

Curriculum areas are identified as arts and crafts; communication; environmental studies; health education; work, leisure and life style; moral reasoning and action; value and belief systems; social, cultural and civic studies; mathematical skills and their applications; scientific and technological ways of knowing and their social applications; health education and environmental studies. The aim is that these core learnings will then be selected and organized by individual schools. (See Figure 3).

Multicultural education in the 1980s: a school's initiative

Finally, in our brief list of examples of and suggestions for multicultural education, I should like to make reference to what one school in the United Kingdom has done to develop multicultural education, for teachers often assume that it is the educationists who are the 'front-runners' and that they themselves do not have the power to innovate.

Birley High School in Manchester has given the lie to that contention (as have many other schools) by publishing details of the

Figure 3
THE CORE LEARNING ENVIRONMENT

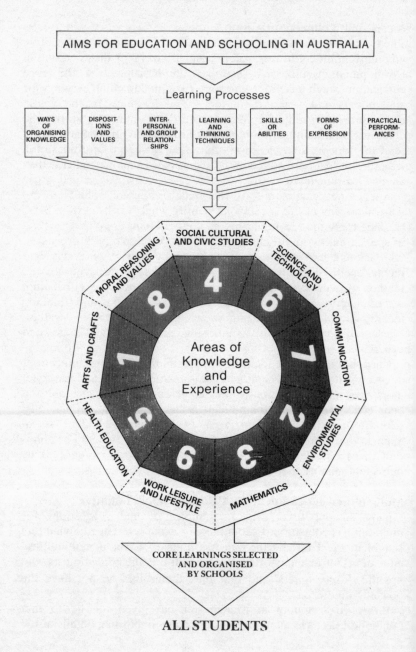

results of the work of a school working party which was set up to look at the whole work and ethos of the school in the light of its multicultural nature, but which, in the event, went far beyond that. After defining multicultural education as a whole curriculum which involves an attitude to life *and* aims to promote a positive self image and respect for the attitudes and values of others, it asserts that, 'Such an education will improve academic attainment'[55] General aims are set out for the school as a whole, curricular aims defined and curriculum discussions described which penetrate into the objectives and content of particular curricular areas. All facets of school life are considered including library policy, in-service training, extra-curricular activities, school assemblies, clubs and groups, minority classes, examinations and teachers' professional activities outside the school. The document attempts to develop a holistic approach in its pursuit of the implications of multiculturalism for an existing institutional and curricular context, seeking permeation of all facets of school life and the articulation of specific criteria and guidelines.

The models considered

Whilst the multicultural curricula, quoted above, have much in common they also have substantial differences. For instance, some of them aim towards the concept of a multiracial society but tend to ignore the multicultural nature of the society where they are located. Others tend to emphasize a particular ethnic contribution, demand or need, whilst others seek to provide for the requirements of the whole population whilst at the same time recognizing special need. Some seek to address particular subject areas within an already existing curriculum whilst others seek a radical reorganization of the epistemology of the school curriculum, imbuing it with the basic values and requirements of a multicultural society.

The importance of these different curricula is not that any one of them is wholly correct or incorrect, but that they represent alternative strategies which can be considered and tested out for their strengths and weaknesses for implementation within the United Kingdom by individual authorities and schools.

In this chapter I have sought to answer the question of how a teacher can begin to construct a more open classroom in the pursuit of multicultural education as part of an overall and ongoing institutional commitment. I have also described briefly a number of conceptualizations of and approaches to multicultural curricula, which others have tried to develop. In the next chapter I want to draw on the strengths of the various positions, strategies and approaches described above, to link them with the theoretical groundwork laid in Chapter One, and to focus them on a model concept of a holistic curriculum for all children within a multicultural society. In doing this, I shall wish to retrieve once again a major theme of Chapter One, namely the need within a multicultural society for a core curriculum supported by a diversity of vocational and cultural options, addressed both to the needs of the whole community and to the special requirements of component cultural groups.

Summary

This chapter has:

1. attempted to draw out some of the major implications of cultural pluralism for the work of the teacher;
2. drawn attention to the dangers of stereotyping, bias in teaching materials and books and bias by omission;
3. argued the need for an open classroom based on dialogical teaching strategies;
4. emphasized the importance of the 'how' of multicultural curriculum development, and given examples of curriculum implementation and content;
5. promised to draw on the material of Chapters One and Two in the definition of a common core curriculum for a multicultural society.

3 A framework for a multicultural curriculum

In Chapter One, I argued that a multicultural curriculum must derive from the ethical and social imperatives of a multicultural society. Put simply, the fundamental ethic is that of 'respect for persons' which implies an intrinsic value for each human being, and the principle of mutuality in rule-making and application. The social imperatives of education are seen to derive predominantly from the fact that our society is democratic, scientific/industrial and offers a broad measure of individual freedom. The reader will recall that these latter were characterized as citizen, worker and person dimensions of the social purposes of education.

It is important to realize that neither the ethical base nor the typification of social purposes corresponds to established subjects or forms of knowledge, nor is the analysis intended in any way to imply that education has only extrinsic value. For like Peters, and in spite of the current unpopularity of the notion, I believe that education does have intrinsic value, that is, it is worthwhile in itself and not because it leads to something else which is of value.[1]

In that same chapter, I have maintained that the implication of providing education in a multicultural society is that we need to agree on a selection from the multiculture which we think is so valuable that we wish it to be handed down, but not solely preserved, in the form of a curriculum. Chapter Two then introduced a few examples of multicultural curricula which gave some idea of what other people have attempted, looking both at the 'how' and the 'what' of curriculum implementation without thereby implying a false separation of content and process.

A system for curriculum design

In this chapter a cultural analysis approach to curriculum planning is adopted, which draws upon and extends the arguments presented in Chapter One. The purpose is to map out certain overall aims for a multicultural curriculum, taking account of some more recent writing in that field, to suggest ways in which a specification of overall shape for the curriculum can be achieved, including knowledge and experience, to identify tentative principles of procedure, including consideration of 'predispositions to learning', and to suggest criteria whereby the whole interrelated system can be monitored and provision made for feedback to its various components.

Figure 4
PRINCIPLES OF PROCEDURE FOR CONSTRUCTING A MULTICULTURAL CURRICULUM

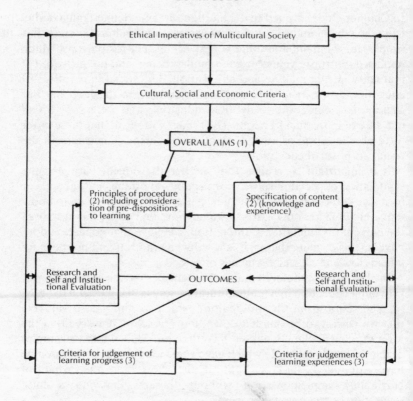

Notes
1. These will include overall aims for the whole curriculum and paradigm aims to guide and secure its multiculturalism.
2. The school and the teacher are constantly monitoring and modifying the process by adapting the procedures and/or adding new content.
3. These include both pupils' and the teacher's evaluation of the judgement.

Although I shall not be dealing with the way in which discourse enters into the construction and monitoring of such a system until Chapter Four, it should be emphasized that what I propose is subject to the overriding principle of provisionality. By that I mean that the whole system and its component parts and functions must be regarded as tentative and provisional, subject to constant 'validity testing' by means of public negotiation between all the parties concerned. This process implies that the curriculum and the underlying principles are both accessible to critical public scrutiny.

Figure 4 illustrates what I have in mind and the kind of steps that I shall be taking in this chapter. It will be obvious that my own thinking in this matter has been considerably influenced by the work of others, some of which has already been referred to in Chapter Two.[2] It is also influenced by the knowledge that a 'clean slate' situation is rare in education and that proposals for what might be, must take account of what is. Moreover, I am not convinced that the response to the challenge of diversity can be a uniform system but rather that taking into account cultural diversity magnifies the professional role and responsibility of the teacher in his community and calls for a maximum flexibility and manoeuvrability for and by the teacher in the service of that community and the broader society. As the London Borough of Brent Teachers Association document well recognizes,

> This is to ask a great deal of teachers. It is to expect that they will in some ways be ahead of our society in general, because there is no doubt that in the population as a whole there is a considerable proportion who are, in some degree, unenthusiastic about the acceptance of minority cultures within the traditional British one. It is to ask teachers to beware of, analyse and discard prejudices which are deep-rooted in our society and others. It is to ask teachers to achieve an understanding of cultures of which they will have had no direct experience in their own lives. These problems from different aspects, face all teachers, white or black.[3]

The intensive dialogue and learning which the above quoted problems demand, endorses the need for pathfinding systems for the negotiation of new knowledge and relationships but counsels the avoidance of rigid rules.

Now, in order to gain purchase on the system which I have proposed and to illustrate its working, I want to ask the question: what is it legitimate for a democratic industrial, multicultural society such as ours, committed to the fundamental ethic of respect for persons, to expect a child on the threshold of formal education to learn before it departs from compulsory education? – for that is tantamount to being the task which teachers as a profession face.

What is it that is so essential to the perpetuation, but not solely the preservation, of our kind of culturally pluralist society, albeit allowing for critical appraisal and often rapid change, that we feel all children must learn, or the alternative result will be that society (and the children) will be inadequately prepared to survive? For an answer to this question, broad aims need to be formulated which will draw on the ethic and the social criteria introduced in Chapter One and provide for the achievement of an element of curriculum continuity from five to 16.

As the Schools Council, in its evidence to the Committee of Inquiry into the Education of Children from Ethnic Minority Groups, succinctly states:

> Education may be justified in a variety of ways; economically, it might be justified on utilitarian grounds, as an input to the production of goods and services; politically, as a means of giving people more control over their roles in society. But in personal terms, it recognizes the capacity of people to be aware, to be curious, to create new ideas, to develop an inner life that becomes richer the more they can make use of the experiences the world has to offer. Education has an obligation to show pupils the diversity of the ways of life devised by man, whether in words, through artefacts, through social organisation, religion or the arts.[4]

The reader will recognize the potential justification for education offered above as the social imperatives, characterized in Chapter One as worker, citizen and person, which form the master aims together with the basic ethic of respect for persons.

These broad aims must now be put into operation, or at least I must try to show how it is possible to put them into operation by indicating the content which would need to be used as the medium for the teaching/learning encounter and the principles which would govern their 'operationalization'. Within the former we shall need to consider both knowledge, or put differently, subject matter, and learning experiences, which transform inert subject matter into the dynamic plane of education praxis; and, in the latter, we need to include principles which not only reflect the ethos of the overall aims but which are, at the same time, attentive to what we know of the ways different children learn: what I have termed, somewhat loosely, predispositions of learning.

Finally, if we are to have any idea at all of what we may have achieved, we require criteria for judging, assessing, monitoring and evaluating outcomes in terms of both intrinsic and extrinsic dimensions and for feedback from that process into the very foundations of the assumptions with which we began and thence throughout the system once again. Put briefly, the sequence is, as reflected in Figure 4, the aims, the content, the principles of procedure and the criteria.

But before we embark on the first part of our journey into the multicultural curriculum, there are two further points to be made. Firstly, whilst, like Stenhouse, I do not find the behavioural objectives model intellectually very satisfactory, the potential application of that model is not excluded from the system which I am proposing, insofar as certain elements of the specification of content may seem to some of my readers to lend themselves to implementation on that basis. I would, in any case, wish to allow for teachers to exercise their particular professional predilection for that choice as an essential element within the emancipatory context of multicultural education. Moreover, it would be utopian to assume that one begins with a *tabula rasa* and any scheme for curriculum reform has to be realistic and practical, both in terms of the individual institution and its style of learning promotion and in terms of the overall ideology of current educational theory, albeit that both are subject to substantial changes over time.

Secondly, it will be important that the principles of procedure take into account what Bruner calls the predispositions to learning, which are likely to comprise the child's 'biography' when it 'crosses the threshold' into formal education.[5] This biography is indispensable to learning strategies in any society but this is particularly so in a multicultural society where cultural experiences prior to entry to school can be so diverse.

This diversity is very testing for the teacher, and it is not easy for him (or her) to become aware of, and make allowance for, the pupil's cultural background, its motivation and personal characteristics and yet avoid the danger of simplistic generalization or even stereotyping. Of course many teachers have been attempting to do just this for some considerable time, taking into account factors such as age, sex, family background, social class, religion and local background and special personal needs. But the increasing complexity of this array of factors makes the discourse with parents and the surrounding community, to which I have previously referred, (and with which I shall deal at greater length in Chapter Four) not just a desirable frill in the education of the child, but an essential prerequisite to successful education. The discourse, if you like, is part of the essential partnership of parents, pupils, teachers and the wider community in the teaching and learning enterprise. But I shall deal with that later.

The aims of multicultural education

Let me return for the moment to the overall aims which form the first stage in building up the model. If we trawl the first two chapters, it will become apparent that there are already a number of items which must be included within the shopping list. To illustrate the process of deriving aims from the ethic and criteria I shall give a few examples of what I mean and show how the chain of deductive reasoning works.

If the major ethic of our society is based on 'respect for persons' this must imply 'respect for oneself'. And both of these in turn imply respect for the culture of others and for one's own. Inherent within both is the idea of mutuality, that is, what I agree applies to you, applies to me as well. For that to be possible the principles proposed have to be public or we could not legitimately expect people to know them. As our society and its knowledge is changing rapidly, they must be subject to what I have termed 'provisionality'. People must become accustomed to uncertainty and to negotiating with each other as a basis for decision and action. For this, people need to develop what I have termed communicative competence, the ability to achieve their rights to power and resources in society by means of a common language and, through that medium, to assist the good of others both economically and socially, whilst contributing to the critical monitoring which alone can provide for humane, rational and ordered change in society. To make such an effective contribution, however, they will require not only the common language but also its specialist registers in the form of science, technology and mathematics. To communicate with others they may need knowledge of other registers too, including foreign ones. But above all they need to be aware of, understand and effectively implement the principles upon which our society is based; the rule of law and quality before it; Western-style parliamentary democracy and political liberty; economic freedom including the right of individuals to strive to improve their financial lot; the right to a private sphere and to personal values and fulfilment; the ability to appraise logically and critically the values by which we live and their implementation.

As you can see I have set up a number of consequential aims which derive from the ethic and social criteria introduced in Chapter One. I hope to have done this without implying that multiculturalism is the only major characteristic which our society possesses, for there are other major social imperatives which will influence both the common core and the alternative components of any curriculum.

The reader will thus be aware that not all the 'incipient' aims to which I have referred refer directly and exclusively to the multicultural nature of our society. Some will derive, for example, from the fact that it is industrial and technological, others from the fact that it is a parliamentary democracy. Moreover, at the moment, whilst the master aims remain common, the derived aims are not ordered. They overlap, do not indicate precedence or relative value, and tend to leave out of account the fact that others have made similar attempts: they smack, in other words, of reinventing the wheel in a rather *ad hoc* fashion.

'Education in Schools: A Consultative Document' (1977)

So let me once again draw on the wisdom of others and refer to efforts which have been made to define the aims of education (or more precisely of schools) within a multicultural society and perhaps to derive a core curriculum from them. Whilst not neglecting earlier work, let us start with the Consultative Document which was issued by the Government in 1977, for it is probably the first official attempt since the 1944 Education Act to ask what the purposes of schools might be and how a coherent and balanced educational experience might be made available to pupils in their period of compulsory schooling. The document identifies eight aims as follows:

i.   To help children develop lively, enquiring minds; giving them the ability to question and to argue rationally, and to apply themselves to tasks.

ii.   To instil respect for moral values, for other people and for oneself, and tolerance of other races, religions, and ways of life.

iii. To help children understand the world in which we live, and the interdependence of nations.

iv.   To help children to use language effectively and imaginatively in reading, writing and speaking.

v.   To help children to appreciate how the nation earns and maintains its standard of living and properly to esteem the essential role of industry and commerce in this process.

vi.   To provide a basis of mathematical, scientific and technical knowledge, enabling boys and girls to learn the essential skills needed in a fast-changing world of work.

vii. To teach children about human achievement and aspirations in the arts and sciences, in religion, and in the search for a more just social order.

viii. To encourage and foster the development of the children whose social or environmental disadvantages cripple their capacity to learn, if necessary by making additional resources available to them.[6]

There is, unfortunately, no time here to give a complete exegesis of the above aims and their shortcomings and, in any case, our task is to look especially to the adequate representation of multicultural dimensions within any such set of aims. But, for a start, this is not a bad set of aims, given a certain degree of overlap and confusion, the absence of any active commitment to the development of education for capability, for craftsmanship, and some 'old-fashioned' rather authoritarian language, such as 'instil'. To continue briefly, with a few examples: aim vi is addressed solely to the world of work, but the areas of knowledge specified could as well address the needs of the citizen or person. Aims i and iv could with advantage be combined for, to my mind, aim i gives a focus and purpose that is otherwise missing. In aim ii, the concept of 'instilling' moral values seems to me too closed, for it assumes a constancy and certainty, closure and a commitment to an apparently indoctrination-style of learning, which does not satisfy me or the criterion of provisionality which I mentioned previously. Similarly 'to esteem the essential role of industry...' is an aim which could lead to a one-sided view.

On the other hand, with all of its shortcomings, aim ii does almost show an awareness of the need to educate for cultural pluralism and the following aim seeks to set this in a global context. True, the aims are rather passive and do not seem to imply preparation for active engagement for the ethic of a multicultural society, but they are a start.

Taken together, these kinds of points seem to me to be symptomatic of the lack of what White has called the overall picture of an educated pupil which one would expect to lie behind such aims – the lack of 'master aims' and of lower order aims to set them in context, which is by far the biggest flaw in this set of aims.

The School Curriculum' (1981)

But we also have a shorter, more recent and, according to the Department of Education and Science and The Welsh Office, more widely accepted set of aims, for in March 1981, the two Government Departments published their long-awaited document on the school curriculum. The number of aims had by that time been reduced to six: no doubt in the interests of economy. These aims were formulated as follows:

1. To help pupils to develop lively, enquiring minds, the ability to question and argue rationally and to apply themselves to tasks, and physical skills.
2. To help pupils to acquire knowledge and skills relevant to adult life and employment in a fast-changing world.
3. To help pupils to use language and number effectively.
4. To instil respect for religious and moral values, and tolerance of other races, religions, and ways of life.

5. To help pupils to understand the world in which they live, and the interdependence of individuals, groups and nations.
6. To help to appreciate human achievements and aspirations.[7]

We should note additionally that three 'issues' are commended to schools for consideration in their curriculum planning and implementation and that one of these major issues is described by the document to be the fact that our society has become a multicultural one.

In general, however, the reader will note the overall similarities in this list and note, as White has pointed out, that we face similar difficulties of lack of master aims, overlap and lack of appreciation of lower order and higher order priority as in the previous example.[8] So really they do not take us very far in either of our quests, namely overall aims for a common core curriculum for all children 5–16 and clarification of the multicultural dimensions which must permeate that curriculum. But they do give us a start along the way.

The Australian core curriculum document, 1980

So let us see if useful ideas can be gathered from other, non-British sources. For my next example, I want to go back to the Australian Curriculum Development Centre document again and see how it tackles this problem of formulating broad overall aims. What we are looking for is a set of aims which will derive from the fundamental ethic of our society (or a society similar to it) and be attentive to the personal, social and economic good of all: a set of aims, which, if implemented, could produce the 'autonomous individual' who can reflect on the reasons underlying his own opinions and behaviour, who can be co-operative and critical in a principled way, measured against the ethic and social criteria, who can be creative in a number of media, and who is affirmatively engaged for reflective change in himself and the wider society.

In the Australian document the following are cited as being amongst the fundamental universal aims of education:

1. The nurturing and development of the powers of reasoning, reflective and critical thinking, imagining, feeling and communicating among and between persons.
2. The maintenance, development and renewal (and not merely the preservation) of the culture; that is of our forms and systems of thought, meaning and expression—such as scientific knowledge, the arts, languages and technology.
3. The maintenance, development and renewal (and not merely the preservation) of the social, economic and political order—including its underlying values, fundamental structures and institutions.

4. The promotion of mental, physical, spiritual and emotional health in all people.[9]

This statement of aims is then backed up by an articulation of major values in Australian society.

Australian society sustains and promotes a way of life which values, inter alia:

1. A sense of personal, group and national identity and unity in all its people.
2. Free communication amongst and between individuals and groups.
3. Responsible participation in community and civic affairs.
4. Tolerance and concern for the rights and beliefs of others.
5. Equality of access to and employment of education, health, welfare and other community services.
6. Self-reliance, initiative and enterprise.
7. Personal and social achievement.
8. Rights to the ownership and use of property including property in the form of personal labour.
9. Productive and socially responsible work.
10. Conservation and development of a shared and dynamic heritage.
11. A sense of individual and group identity.
12. Membership of the international community.[10]

A similar set of common values for British society would not be too difficult to identify and would surely include a commitment to: parliamentary democracy; the rule of law; political, social and cultural pluralism; the right to education; the right to private property; a commitment to a mixed economy; the use of the English language as the main medium of communication; the freedom of the individual; equality of educational opportunity.

Some of these may be more central and indispensable than others; some may even be more subject to dispute than others; but that there is a core of common values that holds us together as a nation state is indisputable.

As the document quite rightly states, it may not be a complete set of aims. For instance, a question might be posed as to whether the environmental dimension is adequately represented. The list does, however, provide a framework within which schools can negotiate their curriculum objectives and it also provides the means to move towards an outline core curriculum for schools, considered holistically. To that extent, it is, to my mind, more rather than less satisfactory than the two examples previously cited. So, in the spirit of provisionality which pervades this book let us use these aims as a tentative basis to set us on our way. So where do we go from here?

Testing aims for their multiculturalism

The next step, it seems to me, is to strain the above aims for their 'multicultural sensitivity'. In other words we need to collect together and amplify the multicultural components of the aims so that they fully reflect the ethical imperative and social purposes of education in a society such as ours, insofar as that relates to multiculturalism, and at the same time provide a touchstone against which teachers can select the material, medium and message of their teaching. To achieve this I propose to build up a set of aims for multicultural education, which, whilst not embracing the breadth of the Australian aims for education and the construction of a core curriculum, encapsulate the essence of what we must aim for if the core curriculum is to be faithful to our multicultural society and provide scope for appropriate alternatives as well.

In this respect, reference should be made to the objectives generated by the Schools Council Project 'Education for a Multiracial Society', which will help to carry us on our way. Readers will recall that the project was carried out at the National Foundation for Educational Research between 1973 and 1976. After the publication of an initial report in 1973[11] and considerable controversy surrounding an aborted final report in 1980, an abridged report finally appeared in 1981, but was unfortunately immediately disowned by its authors.[12] This report, whilst tailoring its objectives to suit its brief slightly more narrowly than our concern in this book and addressing only one aspect of preparation for our multicultural society, namely multiracial education, nonetheless proposes a clarification of objectives which is worth reproducing (see Figure 5 below). The objectives suggested are based on the traditional separation into cognitive (both knowledge and skills) and affective areas, with an acknowledgement of the distinction drawn by Eisner between instructional objectives, which can be prespecified and where the teacher may make the final decision, and expressive objectives, where only the learning situation can be prespecified because the outcomes will be subject to discourse between the learner and the teacher, where each may form their own opinions and conclusions.[13]

More recently the Schools Council issued amended curriculum guidelines for selecting learning experiences for a multicultural curriculum on which we can also draw:

1. The curriculum needs to be both international in its choice of content and global in its perspective.
2. Contemporary British society contains a variety of cultural groups. This

Figure 5
THE OBJECTIVES OF MULTICULTURAL EDUCATION

A Respect for Others
Cognitive (Knowledge)

A1.1 the basic facts of race and racial difference;

A1.2 the customs, values and beliefs of the main cultures represented in Britain and, more particularly, of those forming the local community;

A1.22 why different groups have immigrated to Britain in the past and, more particularly, how the local community has come to acquire its present ethnic composition.

Cognitive (Skills)

All pupils should be able to

A2.1 distinguish fact from opinion and assess the factual content in what they see, hear and read;

A2.2 evaluate their own cultures dispassionately.

Affective (Attitudes, Values and Emotional Sets)

All pupils should accept

A3.1 the uniqueness of each individual human being;

A3.2 the underlying humanity we all share;

A3.3 the principles of equal rights and justice;

A3.4 and value the achievements of other cultures and nations;

A3.5 strangers without feeling threatened;

A3.61 that Britain is a multiethnic society;

A3.62 that no culture is ever static and that constant mutual accommodation will be required of all cultures making up an evolving multicultural society like Britain;

A3.71 that prejudice and discrimination are widespread in Britain and the historical and socioeconomic causes which have given rise to them;

A3.72 the damaging effect of prejudice and discrimination on the rejected groups;

A3.8 the possibility of developing multiple loyalties.

B Respect for Self
Cognitive (Knowledge)

All pupils should know

B1.1 the history and achievements of their own culture and what is distinctive about it.

Cognitive (Skills)

All pupils should be able to

B2.1 communicate efficiently in English and, if it is not their mother tongue, in their own mother tongue;

B2.2 master the other basic skills necessary for success at school.

Affective (Attitudes, Values and Emotional Sets)

All pupils should have developed

B3.1 a positive self-image

B3.2 confidence in their sense of their own identities.[14]

variety should be made evident in the novels, stories and information offered to children.

3. Pupils should have access to accurate information about differences and similarities between cultural groups.

4. People from British minority groups and from other cultures overseas should be presented as individuals with every variety of human quality and attribute. Stereotypes of minority groups in Britain and of cultures overseas, whether expressed in terms of human characteristics, life styles, social roles or occupational status, are unacceptable and likely to be damaging.

5. Other cultures and nations have their own values; whenever possible they should be allowed to speak for themselves so that they can be better understood, and not judged in terms of British or European norms.[15]

A set of paradigm multicultural aims

The above objectives, the aims specified in the Australian document and the common core values of British society identified above, give us a useful springboard to the kind of 'validity testing' aims (or guidelines) for teachers which we are seeking to set at the side of the overall aims, and they put us in a position to be able to articulate such aims slightly more closely. So let us try to agree on a set of provisional working aims for multicultural education.

A paramount aim must be to produce the autonomous individual who is yet a 'respecter of persons'. He or she must be in a position critically to reflect on the prime movers of his or her opinions and actions to test them out for their mutuality, accepting that what is right and just for him must be accepted as right and just for others, and for their congruence with the basic ethic of respect for persons.

Secondly, and to achieve the first aim, the individual will need the abilities of communicative competence, both in spoken and written form and through a number of modes including verbal, numerical and artistic. In implementation, this aim will certainly require a baseline of knowledge, a high level of critical and reflective thinking, conceptual sophistication and logical reasoning appropriate to the age and ability of the individual, and the capacity to engage in sensitive and creative dialogue with others in pursuit of information, in the eradication of misunderstanding, and in a process of interlearning where cultural exchange can take place with those of a different cultural background.

In practice and in content this implies excellence in the *lingua franca* and development, not just maintenance, of mother tongue competence. Symbiotic with the aim of communicative competence is the area of social skills which will enable the individual to develop effective interchange relationships within and across groups as well as between individuals. Intercultural competence has both cognitive and affective dimensions which will enable the individual to accept the rejection of his or her own ideas.[16]

Again linked to the latter aim must be the development not only of tolerance and concern for the rights and beliefs of others, but a commitment to practical engagement for them. This includes for instance, not just an ˋabhorrence of racism, prejudice and discrimination, but involvement in active measures to combat them.

Fifthly, and in pursuit of the last aim, the person will need the knowledge, skills and expertise to participate effectively in both community and wider political matters, willing to accept responsibility for the affairs of others (and election, if appropriate) and attentive to the imperative of accountability in that responsibility.

Acceptance of the need for systematic, deliberate and rational change will have to be allied to this commitment to the political life of the society, if it is not to stagnate. But this acceptance itself requires linking with a sensitive, even compassionate, understanding of the fact that, faced with the need to change, minorities must have extra safeguards and rights, and that first and foremost amongst these must be the rights of individuals and groups to preserve their cultural and social identity, insofar as this contributes to the multiculture of our society and is not in conflict with its basic ethic and principles.

Associated with this capability, internally within British society, individuals need to be able to set that in a more global context, cherishing their membership of a wider international community and shunning racial, national, religious and other stereotypes, whilst understanding how easy it is to indulge ethnocentric feelings as an 'instant' mechanism to explain and replace rationality.

Finally, the individual will require cognitive knowledge to sustain the expressive/affective commitments and engagement listed above. To repeat what I said in Chapter One, it is unreasonable to expect people to respect that which they do not know and understand. It will therefore be essential that the individual has a cultural chart of his or her own society and of the broader global context which includes an awareness both of the roots from which grow the racism of his or her own society and of the political, economic and social systems of which he or she is a part, and his or her own responsibility to and for them. Interpreted to the level of content this must include knowledge of our society and a broader awareness of issues such as the distribution of power and access to resources in it.

All these aims will need to be subject to an overriding aim to foster the critical acceptance of uncertainty and provisionality in human knowledge and understanding and of the partial and tentative nature of human cognition and interaction.

Aims for a multicultural curriculum will need to be scrutinized to make sure they include the above at least.

The content of the multicultural curriculum

Bearing in mind that the theme of this book is the multicultural curriculum, and that multiculturalism is only one of the imperatives (though to my mind the most important one) which should influence the aims, shape, content and process of compulsory education (and referring back to Figure 4 which gives a chart of the journey we are currently undertaking), it will be clear to the reader that our next two tasks are the specification of content, both knowledge and experiences, and the identification of the guiding principles including consideration of predispositions to learning. Further, whilst I shall try to present ideas for the design and provision of a core holistically, we shall need to refocus from time to time, jettisoning material which is relevant more broadly to the core, for example its scientific and technological dimensions, its craftsmanship dimensions, its environmental dimensions etc., in order to keep more closely to our 'multicultural course'. We shall also need to keep in mind that it is unlikely that exactly the same curriculum will be appropriate for a school in Bradford as for schools in Brighton, in Sunderland or in Swansea.

Having defined our master aims for multicultural education, we come to the question of the overall shape of a multicultural curriculum, including the knowledge and learning processes which will enable us to address the kind of aims discussed above. To recap, what we are saying is that teachers need to include, in all learning strategies, curricula, pedagogies, materials, examinations and organization modes which will deliberately seek to embrace and actively respond to the diversity of cultures represented in our society, whether of age, sex, religion, occupation, social class, ethnic origin, race, religion or language or combinations of these, such as ethclass[17] whilst at the same time emphasizing and reinforcing the common core values of that society (this applies both to subject matter and teaching/learning strategies). Both diversity and commonality of our multiculture will need to be available both in the form of common learning (concerned both with diversity and commonality) and in the form of special provision.

But let me give some examples to illustrate what I mean. To set us on our journey, it is worthwhile reminding ourselves once again of the challenge to the school and teachers which the newly perceived

commitment to multicultural education involves. As the Schools
Council's view of multicultural education makes clear:

> In a society which believes in cultural pluralism, the challenge for
> teachers is to meet the particular needs of pupils from different religious,
> linguistic and ethnic sub-cultures; to prepare *all* pupils for life in a world
> where they will meet, live and work with fellow citizens of diverse
> religions, languages and ethnic origins; and also to seize the opportunity
> to enrich the lives of all their pupils by taking account of the cultural
> diversity around them.[18]

The major dimensions of this task, which we might characterize for
the moment as special provision for all against a background of
cultural diversity within our (unitary) society, represents an
interacting network of factors which are fundamental to curriculum
construction in a multicultural society. Each school must seek to
make provision for special needs related both to the diversity and to
the underlying unity of our society. The examples given are of purely
cognitive/knowledge, instructional dimensions, but they could as
easily have been chosen from the cognitive/skills of affective/
expressive areas with the proviso that the latter area is less
susceptible to the specification of learning objectives.

Mother-tongue teaching and learning is clearly not of importance
to all pupils but it is an aspect of legitimate culture which it is
desirable for economic, political and not least cultural reasons to
seek to perpetuate. English is the indispensable medium through
which the common culture is transmitted and regenerated and
therefore all pupils must have a high level of communicative
competence and this may imply a special need for those whose
mother-tongue is not English. Similarly, and conversely, knowledge
of the basic ethic of British society (and of active engagement for its
creative preservation) are essential to all pupils, as is a knowledge
chart of its diversity and a commitment to preserve it creatively. Thus
it is not a simple matter of multiculture=special provision,
commonality=whole school provision, which is the deficit model of
multicultural education, but an overlapping grid of interaction
between these four factors, as illustrated in Figure 6.

It will be apparent from the proposed model that curriculum content,
to be faithful to our multicultural society, needs to embrace a core of
common learnings related both to the unity and diversity of that
society, and alternative additionals which enable response to special
needs related to the cultural factors mentioned above and
combinations of them such as social class and ethnicity (or ethclass)
related to age, sex, etc. (and this applies to the pedagogy as much as

to the subject matter). It is important to emphasize that multiple-factor consideration is inherent within and essential to the concept of a multicultural curriculum in action, for, in a pluralist society, single-factor explanatory models are unlikely to achieve sufficient purchase on issues to have more than a simplistic (and largely apparent) explanatory value which can itself mislead. Moreover they imply a stability and perseverance that is not realistic. It is for this reason also that I share Stenhouse's dislike of the use of the term subculture to describe the multiple but fluid membership of changing groups which characterizes our society and its cultural make-up.[19]

Figure 6
A SIMPLIFIED MODEL OF CURRICULUM ISSUES

Kind of provision for Pupils \ Responding to needs generating by	Diversity and Pluralism	Commonality and Common Values
Whole School Provision	e.g. knowledge of the British multiculture	e.g. knowledge of the basic ethic of British society
Special Provision	e.g. mother-tongue learning	e.g. communicative competence in English

The above points are of importance for the teacher to bear in mind both in the selection of curriculum knowledge and learning experiences and also for the principles of procedure, including predispositions to learning. The bridge between these two pairs of concepts is the pedagogy or teaching strategies, which link the principles of procedure as the guidelines for implementation to the content that is the medium to be used. But let us for the moment return to the question of the content of the multicultural curriculum, recognizing both knowledge and learning experiences as important components to be considered.

Firstly, let us take the content of education, whilst remembering that schools, contrary to historical perceptions, are not usually manufacturers of knowledge but rather the retail outlets where small, highly selected, packaged samples are distributed to the coming generation of adults, according to the criteria generated by the system of social stratification. That means, as Musgrave points out, that 'knowledge and its representation in the curriculum is stratified in ways deeply dependent upon the power structure'.[20] This, in turn, must imply that any proposal for a multicultural curriculum has to reckon with the political context within which it is to be implemented, national, local and institutional, although to differing degrees and in different ways, and it must be sensitive to the distribution of power and resource which locks the school curriculum into place in relation to the system of social stratification. (In passing we must also note that both these latter are constantly changing in themselves and in their relationship to each other).

For these reasons, it is important to allow for strategies which recognize that 'there are many roads to Rome' and many variants on achieving a multicultural curriculum, some of which have been described in Chapter Two. Thus, whether we favour a Hirstian curriculum theory recognizing forms of knowledge such as mathematics and formal logic, physical sciences, human sciences including history, religion, aesthetics, philosophy and moral understanding,[21] a traditional subject-based one, a skill-based one, one grounded in areas of experience, one derived from the dynamic concept of 'knowledge constitutive interests'[22] as propounded by Habermas, or some alternative, it is inherent in our multicultural curriculum that it must arise from what exists, whilst recognizing the inadequacy of that and the urgent need for radical change. Additionally, however, it must offer a holistic means of appraising and making decisions on a programme of learning to be offered to a child during its progression through compulsory schooling.

Having said that, it is possible to set up a checklist, ideal-type common core of curriculum content, which is not an invitation to uniformity or prescription for conformity, but which can be used as a yardstick to gauge the need for change in existing curricula. This is what I now propose to do.

The Department of Education and Science, the Inspectorate, the Welsh Office and the Scottish Education Department have all made recent attempts to define the essential learnings necessary for all individuals if they are to be considered educated. The Assessment of Performance Unit, established within the DES in 1974, in its search for a means of looking across the curriculum on an other than straight subject basis, identified six areas: verbal, mathematical, scientific, ethical, aesthetic and physical, which were later amended. But the invocation is quite clearly to a more than 'collection', that is accumulation of existing subjects, basis for looking at the curriculum.[23]

Probably the strongest representation of the need for a common baseline for all pupils is that presented in the *Curriculum 11-16* document, which actually discusses constructing a common curriculum comprising certain essential areas of experience: the aesthetic and creative, the ethical, the linguistic, the mathematical, the physical, the scientific, the social and political, the spiritual.[24] The intention of the two examples cited above is to offer scope for curricular analysis and construction, which defines the areas in which all pupils should have progressive experience if they are to be educated. It is at the same time a check on completeness as well as on continuity across compulsory education which can be responded to by schools according to their analysis of their skills and expertise, their cultural context and the needs of their clients. Although, in general, the spirit and intention of the above proposals are tenable, one or two alterations might make them more consistent. The ethical and spiritual, for instance, might be regarded as a single domain and 'creative' could be an adjective applied to all domains and not just the aesthetic.

If we look again at the Australian document, we see that it also eschews the idea of a curriculum seen as no more than a set of compulsory subjects and proposes a core which embraces subject matter, teaching/learning processes and learning situations organized around a set of aims, principles and values related to the defined characteristics and major needs of contemporary society. It suggests that the basic learning tools and resources should include: communicating in spoken and written language; number skills, mathematical reasoning and spatial relationships; scientific processes and their applications; logical inquiry and analysis; creative, imaginative and intuitive ways of thinking and experiencing; the capacity to apply and use knowledge symbols, processes and skills; perception, expression and appreciation through the arts and crafts; manual and other physical skills; management of bodily and mental health; the personal articulation of experience and thinking into value and belief systems.[25]

It then proposes a set of seven learning processes and nine areas of knowledge and experience as follows: arts and crafts, environmental studies, health education; scientific and technological ways of knowing and their applications; communication; moral reasoning and action; and, work, leisure and lifestyle.[26] Core learning processes, by means of which that subject matter may be achieved, could include: learning and thinking techniques, ways of organizing knowledge; dispositions and values; skills or abilities; forms of expression; practical performances; interpersonal and group relationships.[27]

These learning processes, selected in a fairly random way, could be expressed along a continuum from pure abstraction such as verbalization and concept formation in literature, to direct, purposeful and concrete experience such as skill development in technology. They could range from hearing about the caste system on the Indian subcontinent and discussing it as part of the process of discussion of social stratification, to cooking and eating an Indian meal and thus learning to be gastronomically more catholic.

Although it must be emphasized that there may be many different ways of achieving the kinds of aims which have been outlined and proposed in this chapter, a combination of the 11-16 'subject matter tally' and the Australian approach to the identification of core learning processes seems one efficacious means of starting the process of dialogue which results in the more specific subject matter, expressed in syllabuses, sequencing of learning experiences, and modes of experience appropriate to the learning styles of individual children. The core subject matter and learning processes might, for example, be summarized as in Figure 7.

Figure 7
A CORE CURRICULUM AND LEARNING PROCESSES

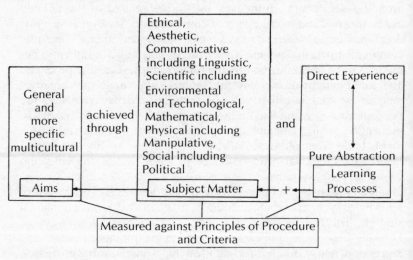

A few immediate points of explanation should be made about the model. Firstly, some of the aims may be achieved by direct, purposeful experience in the subject matter areas identified, by means of the learning processes indicated. Thus, a pupil may learn to speak or to woodcarve or to swim by direct encounter with the elements concerned, language, materials and tools, water, and through one or more of the learning processes. On the other hand, he may experience some of the subject matter only indirectly by the proxy of someone else's spoken, visual or other stimuli. He may for instance never see Australia and will experience it vicariously by means of books, films, etc. He may live in an area where there are few ethnic minority group members and pupils and yet meet them every day in his classroom through the books and visuals used in the classroom.

In this respect, I have often found Dale's conceptualization of the 'cone of experience' to be of use in exemplifying a range of human learning processes available along the continuum from direct experience to pure abstraction.[28] Secondly, although it is clear that the model requires further refinement, the sequencing and systematization may be found helpful where reference is made to other published materials dealing with particular and sometimes alternative formulations and components often produced for a different purpose.[29] For instance, instead of my formulation of subject matter, some readers may prefer that of Gagné, where he answers the question of what is learned with a five-part categorization, as follows: intellectual skills, cognitive strategies, verbal information, motor skills and attitudes.[30] Thirdly, the model is intended to leave schools and teachers sufficient flexibility and manoeuvrability to make their own decisions, but to be able to justify their reasons for these decisions in a wider context and if necessary to a wider audience. Fourthly, as it was necessary with the aims to glean the elements directly relevant to a multicultural education, so also it is necessary to identify those core elements of subject matter and learning experience which enable us to achieve the multicultural aims in particular, and here there will inevitably be a difference in weighting. No one goal, for instance, is likely to be attainable via one element of subject matter and one process.

Finally, there is still a need to define and identify those core learnings which are indispensable to a core curriculum which is truly part of a multicultural education. Whilst there will be many alternative views, these must surely include both cognitive and affective dimensions addressed to such areas of competence as:

A commitment to value and actively support the culturally diverse nature of society;

A critical awareness of and pride in oneself and one's own culture insofar as it is congruent with the basic ethics of society;

An accurate and factual knowledge of the British multiculture, the commonalities of British society and the richness and diversity of representative cultures;

A commitment to active engagement for, and in respect for others, their cultures and lifestyles insofar as they are in line with the basic ethics of society and particularly for the improvement of race relations;

An ability to live with the paradox of practising cultural sensitivity, whilst treating each person as an individual;

Communicative competence over a range of registers and with a variety of cultural groups;

Intercultural competence, that is the ability to relate creatively to individuals and groups of a different cultural background and to 'interlearn' with them;

An awareness of, and competence in, a variety of aesthetic forms and media reflective of the diversity available in society;[31]

A knowledge of the social, educational and economic systems and the way in which they contribute to racial and other cultural discrimination;

A sensitive awareness of the sources of bias, discrimination and prejudice in British society, identifying whatever generic descriptions are used, and an ability to combat them, and understand why they are incompatible with the fundamental ethic of our society;

An active ability and willingness to evaluate one's own opinions and behaviour reflexively against the basic ethics of society;

An acceptance of the 'mutuality' of commitment to criteria for such evaluation and to discourse as the means of generating them;

An ability to celebrate difference of view and ability to see one's own opinions rejected;

An active engagement for constructive but humane social change and an acceptance of his/her own role in that change;

A commitment to 'open-mindedness' and the acceptance of uncertainty and provisionality;

An ability to view all their learning, as necessary, in a wider world view, and in a reflexive way which is committed to rational and collaborative improvement.

One example of an attempt to collate such subject matter into what the author calls 'the compulsory core elements' or a 'survival curriculum' for all children in a polyethnic society, offers the following identification of core elements and their relative weighting, and an indication of the contributory subjects and disciplines.[32] Readers might like to reflect on their own current curriculum and measure it against my core content for a multicultural curriculum and Bullivant's attempt to sculpt from similar content a core multicultural curriculum. The same exercise could be applied to the Australian proposal quoted earlier.

Figure 8
CORE ELEMENTS IN THE SURVIVAL CURRICULUM

Core element	Weighting	Contributing subjects and disciplines
A. Communicative Competence	X3	Basic English (including grammar) literatures, historical narrative, graphics, dance, drama, music
B. Political and Economic Competence	X3	Social studies, sociology, economics, politics, commercial studies, recent history
C. Numeracy	X2	Arithmetic, Social numeracy, geometry
D. Moral and Social Education	X1	Social studies, anthropology, philosophy, comparative religion
E. Environmental Awareness	X1	Geography, general science, biology

(Copyright: Bullivant, B., *Race, Ethnicity and Curriculum*, Melbourne: Macmillan, 1981, p.71).

Allied with this core curriculum Bullivant proposes what he calls *enrichment electives,* such as music, drama, creative arts, sports, etc., which focus in particular on the person dimension of our overall aims, in enabling, in particular, children to gain personal satisfaction from their education; and *academic* electives, which are more utilitarian (predominantly worker dimension) which enable children to survive in a highly competitive society, for example economics, sciences etc.

Teachers might like to test out the applicability of Bullivant's model for their school and its cultural context. For instance, does it offer an opportunity for mother tongue teaching to be an integral part of the recognized curriculum within the enrichment electives, in those areas where there is demand for such provision, without that being the case where there is no such demand? Is the core sufficiently reflective of the cognitive and affective dimensions mentioned above? Is it weak on the aesthetic dimension?

Principles of procedure
Teachers must take note of the strictures of Bantock concerning those educationists who make proposals for curriculum design and

development without reference to the differential psychological and social potential of sections of the population, including concept formation, motivation, linguistic and social background.[33]

Certainly, concomitant with a general orthodoxy that the implications of cultural pluralism for education were to be traced through into subject matter, there has been a growing body of evidence accumulating for almost two decades now that differences in achievement between minority and non-minority pupils can be explained in terms that are related to socioeconomic and cultural background. In this respect teachers need to distinguish between performance—that is, observed achievement—and competence—that is, the ability to achieve—which may not manifest itself because of the motivational techniques employed by the teacher or for some other cultural reason. Motivation by the teacher—that is, the means (and will) to gain purchase on the pupil's competence in order to achieve performance—has to be understood in terms of the sociocultural contexts and predispositions of the parties involved and of the proposed learning context. Thus a pupil from an ethnic minority community may be highly motivated and highly competent: but he may be motivated by different factors from those which represent a commonality between the teacher and many 'majority' pupils. Such knowledge has to be translated by the teacher into strategies for learning which liberate all pupils' competence into the form that we call achievement. This implies emancipating them from old-fashioned and discredited *deficit* theories of human ability and building on the divergent experiences, capacities and motivational 'triggers' which will provide a greater equality of opportunity for all.[35] As I understand it, and at the risk of oversimplifying, this is at the base of Maureen Stone's argument that it is not inadequate self concept but rather inadequate pedagogy to which West Indian underachievement must be attributed.[36] As Carrington points out:

> It is well known that teachers generally operate with perceived notions about the patterns of behaviour and the levels of ability of different categories of pupil, and that these stereotypes (which may relate to class, sex or race) not only influence the teachers' attitudes and behaviour towards the categories in question but also the curriculum content and *teaching style* selected. [My italics][37]

It is clear that, in actually teaching a multicultural curriculum, a teacher has to attempt to take into account the immense variety of cognitive styles, of cultural and socioeconomic background, of linguistic competence, of age, etc., and seek to match this with his current (provisional) knowledge of such matters as motivation and learning, whilst avoiding the hidden expectation that all children have the same cognitive style as he or she does and are motivated by the same factors. This is where the principles of procedure achieve their significance, for these are the runway to the implementation of the content, the vehicle for which is the teaching/learning strategies. As such the principles of procedure must be expressive of factors such as those alluded to, psychological, cultural and social. A tentative list might include the following:

1. The teacher will analyse his or her own biases and seek to modify them;
2. The teacher will pursue knowledge of, and increase his or her sensitivity to, the cultural background of his or her pupils;
3. He or she will, however, treat all persons as individuals, seeking to build on the experience and capacities which children bring to school;
4. A climate of acceptance, mutual respect and collaboration will be created facilitating free expression of ideas, feelings and diverse cultural capital;
5. Pupils will be assisted to construct a positive self-image and positive attitudes towards others;
6. Experiences will be developed which help pupils to develop a sensitivity to the needs and feelings of others;
7. A learning environment will be striven for which expresses a co-operative ethic, is conducive to racial harmony, to an understanding and valuing of all cultural groups, and which is 'pedagogically' sensitive to different social and cultural backgrounds;
8. The teaching will express a commitment to the worth and dignity of the individual, and it will avoid stereotypical labelling of the competence of different ethnic groups;
9. Procedures for assessment and evaluation will be fair to all cultural groups;
10. Minority views will be afforded the same critical hearing and appraisal as majority views;
11. A commitment will be manifest to the provisionality of knowledge and the consideration of teaching materials as a source of evidence rather than authority;
12. Constructive social action will be encouraged as supportive of the knowledge of the social, economic and other power structures of society provided;
13. Learning processes will be designed in accord with present knowledge of differences in cognitive functioning, motivation and ethnic background;

14. Materials will be used which are free from cultural bias;
15. The teaching will encourage a high level of rational and reflexive thinking.[38]

Clearly such a list of principles must always remain incomplete, not only in the items listed but in the interpretation of the existing items into the individual school and teacher context. They need careful and sensitive interpretation to match the range of cultural factors including age, sex, ability, social class and ethnic background. Each school and teacher will need to examine the checklist and test it for its validity in their cultural context, as a basis for ongoing reflection about their pursuit of cultural tolerance and equality of educational opportunity. In doing this they will need to generate a series of criteria on the basis of which they can gauge their checklist of procedural principles. This will need to include both teachers and pupils and, if the judgements are to be legitimated in the wider society, the community as well.

Criteria for judgement

It is of the essence of the criteria for judgement that they are the means whereby the system is locked in creative momentum. They are the yardstick against which not only outcomes but also the system itself and its participant's performances are judged. For this reason, if for no other, it is essential that such criteria are regarded as subject to refutation on rational grounds and therefore available for public discourse. In this sense the need is for a process model of evaluation rather than a 'product efficiency' one: one, that is, which goes beyond data, however achieved, to an examination of the values and assumptions underlying that data, and which focuses on the teaching and learning as a whole, set within a particular dynamic, cultural and institutional context but accountable to certain suprainstitutional, cultural ethics.

At this stage we are concerned with criteria for the evaluation of teaching and learning, addressed to the aims outlined in this chapter, which in turn are responsive to the underlying ethic and social imperatives in accord with the principles of procedure. None of this precludes change in any of the elements and the criteria for judgement of teaching and learning presuppose institutional and wider community and systemic policies and criteria, which sustain the commitment to multicultural education. (These wider concerns and criteria are a major concern of the next chapter, Chapter Four).

The guidelines developed and published by the Multiethnic Inspectorate of the Inner London Education Authority provide a very useful exemplar for teachers who would like to see a model of how they can begin to review their school's response to the demands of multicultural education. A checklist is provided for such areas as school policy, equality of opportunity, racism, curriculum, classroom strategies, resources, language, ethos and atmosphere, support and care of pupils, staff development, parents and their communities and school to work. As a starter towards a more sophisticated set of criteria the document is a pathfinder for work in the United Kingdom, and has the advantage of attractive and simple layout.

In the field of developed instruments, that would be suitable for the purpose of overall evaluative criteria, we are probably fairly reliant on American material at the moment. For instance, the National Study of School Evaluation in the United States produced a set of evaluation guidelines for multicultural education as long ago as 1973. In addition to statements of philosophy, objectives and principles for multicultural education, together with criteria to evaluate these, the guidelines offer detailed criteria for appraising the school structure—including the racial balance, attitudes and commitment of staff; the school organization and grouping; the formal curriculum; learning materials; special education and provision; extra-curricular activities; pupil services including pastoral and counselling provision; and decision-making, including pupil and community involvement. The material includes provision for an overall evaluation of the school's involvement in multicultural education, a mechanism to encourage change and a student opinionaire.

A different but similarly detailed evaluation checklist was contained in a position statement of the National Council for the Social Studies published in 1976. This comprises a series of 23 basic criteria, which call the school's educational provision to the bar of a multicultural accountability across areas such as the school ethos, its policies and procedures, the school staff, in-service provision, reflection of different cognitive styles in learning strategies and materials, student self-image, knowledge of the multicultural nature of society, the promotion of values, attitudes and behaviours conducive to multicultural education, education for effective and potent citizenship, interpersonal and interethnic relations, ethnic representativeness of the curriculum coverage, interdisciplinarity and open-mindedness of the curriculum, aesthetic dimension, minority languages, use of local community resources and commitment to ongoing evaluation. Each of these areas is further subdivided into a number of sub-categorizations.

A further example, developed in the United States by the teacher's organization, the National Education Association, is the 'Profile of Excellence' addressed to the establishment of racial equality in schools, and produced in 1980. It addresses six components with a number of criteria which if fulfilled would secure equality of education for all pupils. The six components are called governance and administration, personnel and staffing, curriculum and instruction, school facilities, student services and school community relations.

For the purposes of this chapter it is worth giving further detail of the third case, curriculum and instruction, where a definition is given of curriculum and instruction and the underlying assumptions concerning racial equality are made explicit. There is then a checklist of criteria for adequacy of excellence, after which the teacher is asked to respond as to whether they are adequate, excellent or deficient. Specific evidence is asked for as justification for the response given and an explanation requested for deficiencies cited. Finally, a request for recommendations for improvement is included. The curricular and instructional areas covered include the availability of a school policy statement, the involvement of persons of different racial backgrounds, provision of in-service education, attentiveness to the racial and cultural identities of pupils, racism and its effects. Whilst this last example is by no means as detailed as the other two cited, in technique it may appeal to teachers more, for it is more open-ended and invites participation in reflecting on answers, identifying strengths and weaknesses and proposing deliberate strategies for change.

To return to the United Kingdom again, Schools Council Programme One on 'Purpose and Planning in Schools' has resulted in a very useful publication which could help schools to generate their own criteria and to evaluate their provision according to them. It gives a classification of strategies for introducing self-evaluation, based on initiatives taken by LEAs, but emphasizes the need for a school to pick up the idea of evaluation, to internalize it and to make the process its own, responsive to its own unique features.

This seems to me the essence of both the generation of criteria and the other components of the model which I have tried to offer in this chapter. Some will feel that firmer, more programmatic guidance should have been given on the criteria and on the other parts of the model. But each model and each set of criteria has its strengths and weaknesses. The important thing is that each offers one means for a school and its teachers to build and to test out their commitment to multicultural education, its principles and implementation in their own institution and classroom. Only if they internalize it and make it their own will it have their necessary commitment. Thus the documents cited in the Notes to this chapter fulfil the requirement of tentative 'pathfinder' criteria for the monitoring and evaluation of the model proposed earlier in the chapter. As such they are subject to reasoned amendment on a collegial and hopefully community basis.

We have travelled a long way in this chapter, from the point where we began by incorporating the ethic and social imperatives into a formulation of aims for multicultural education, to the point in the last section, where I have proposed a means to evaluate the extent to which we as teachers actually live up to these ideals in our daily practice. In the next chapter, we seek to set the teacher's responsibility for multicultural education in a wider community and societal context, looking at issues such as school management practices for multicultural education and the forging of a real partnership of diversity in pursuit of the goals of multicultural education.

Summary

This chapter has:

1. outlined a system for multicultural curriculum design;
2. discussed some recent proposals for the aims of education and schools and suggested a set of paradigm multicultural aims against which they can be tested;
3. proposed an overall shape for a core curriculum and some essential learnings for its multicultural content;
4. suggested a continuum of learning processes from direct experience to pure abstraction;
5. offered a series of principles of procedure for the implementation of a multicultural curriculum;
6. described in outline three sets of criteria for judging multicultural curricula in particular;
7. drawn attention to the content of the next chapter and its relationship to this chapter.

4 The community and the multicultural school

In the preceding three chapters, I have referred often to the need for discourse in the development of multicultural education. In Chapter One, it was seen as the means whereby the fundamental ethic of a society such as ours and the social imperatives were made actual in the functioning of education. In Chapter Two, it was presented as the means by which alone the teacher could take account of a bewildering array of diversity, of which teachers may themselves never have direct experience; and, in Chapter Three it was argued to be the fundamental means whereby important negotiations concerning the design, implementation and monitoring of a multicultural curriculum could be effected.

In this chapter I want to define more closely what I mean by discourse and use a tentative working definition as a vehicle to identify the kinds of home-school, parent-teacher, school-community relations on which alone a multicultural commitment can be predicated.

School and community: the developing partnership

Of course, it is important not to give the impression that nothing has yet been done. For years we have known that encouragement in the home and the presence of appropriate home circumstances contribute substantially to the achievement of the school's academic goals. The importance of the parental role and attitudes in education and of home circumstances was gradually unveiled in the years after the introduction of secondary education for all. The Central Advisory Council's report in 1954 indicated the far-reaching influence of the home background and the Newsom Report of 1963 focused lay and professional opinion on the fact that 'The schools cannot do the job alone..... Many situations would be helped simply by the schools knowing more of the home circumstances and the parents knowing more of what goes on in the school'. It recommended that 'there is urgent need to strengthen all existing links between home and school, and in difficult areas to create new ones....'[2]

Schools Council *Enquiry 1* pointed out that one of the ways that those who left school early differed from those who did not was their home background, with the physical conditions and resources tending to be unconducive in the case of the former group, and significantly in view of the theme of this book, it referred to the absence in their homes of a tradition of extended education and the consequent imperfect understanding of the aims and methods of teaching[3] But it was the Plowden Report which first fully endorsed the partnership between home and school on which full support for children's endeavours depended, when it stated:

> It has long been recognised that education is concerned with the whole man; henceforth it must be concerned with the whole family[4]

The 1960s saw a massive increase in interest in education, expressed in the establishment of organizations such as the Pre-School Playgroup Association in 1961, the first Association for the Advancement of State Education in the same year and the National Confederation for the Advancement of State Education in 1962, the Advisory Centre for Education in Cambridge in 1963, through such organizations as the Home-School Council to the foundation in 1970 of the National Association of Governors and Managers.

By the early 1970s, a Schools Council research project on *Parents and Teachers* could report that '…most experienced teachers realize the vital role played by the home in successful child education, but (that) they sometimes fail to recognize the influential role they themselves can play in determining the attitude of parents to the education of their children'; and further, emphasizing the implications for curriculum, '. . . a great deal can be done to integrate the school more firmly with the local community through a deep involvement of the curriculum with the environment in which the children have grown up and developed.' Significantly too, the report pointed to the fact that parents of non-British background tended to visit the school less frequently than others[5]

But movement towards strategies to include such parents, indeed parents at all, were slow and the Bullock Report had to point out diplomatically that

> There are good arguments for a more sustained and systematic service linking home and school, especially in the areas of intensive immigrant settlement. [6]

Going straight to the core of the issue it recommended that

The role of members of the minority communities themselves is vital and it is particularly important that children from families of overseas origin should see people of their own communities in the role of teacher and helper.[7]

The same year as the Bullock Report was published a Committee of Enquiry was appointed to review 'the arrangements for the management and government...of schools...their relationships... with parents of pupils and with the local community at large'.[8]

One minority report pointed out trenchantly that

Whilst the Committee has been sitting further interest has been engendered, and to some extent the fires of controversy fuelled by the Tyndale affair, the events in Tameside, the Prime Minister's Ruskin speech, the so-called 'Yellow Paper', the Bennett Report on 'Teaching Styles and Pupil Progress', and the debates and discussions relating to the proposed common examination at 16+ and the question of the core curriculum. It is clear to me that parents and the community in general, to a very considerable extent, have lost confidence in our schools.[9]

In face of this the Committee's recommendations, though alarming to some, can only be described as anodyne, based on a continuing hierarchical concept of relationships between pupils and teachers and school and community. Whilst the special problems of minority communities might not have existed as far as the Committee was concerned, even its recommendation that

The Governing Body should satisfy itself that adequate arrangements are made to inform parents, to involve them in their children's progress and welfare, to enlist their support, and to ensure their access to the school and a teacher by reasonable arrangement.[10]

did little to move towards the concept of a partnership which legally, morally and functionally was what was being increasingly demanded. Even its recommendation concerning the setting of aims for a school by the governing body was confined to the consideration to be given to constructive suggestions from any individuals or organizations with a concern for the school's welfare, rather than the parents and community who provide the children, the resources and the cultural capital – at least of the parallel curriculum.

Little wonder then that already at that time research was seeming to indicate the fact that teachers were unaware in many cases of the bicultural capital with which this parallel curriculum endowed children, and that this state inhibited them from understanding the problems of minority children, with a consequent withdrawal of those children into their own culture.[11] But the withdrawal appeared to be mutual, for teachers also seemed to be developing 'coping strategies' which enabled them to ignore and avoid ethnic minority children![12] It is not surprising that the consequent exclusion of minority culture and of minority communities from influence on, and participation in, schools results in considerable underachievement[13] and the generation of theories to account for that underachievement which emphasize hereditary factors rather than historical or social forces![14] Certainly, where ethnic minority communities are deprived of potent access to and participation in the opportunity structure at its 'first base' level, that is, the education system, it is not surprising if their representation at later stages is minimal, a situation contributing to the problems of a society, overtly committed to equality of opportunity, which rests paradoxically on a 'caste system' of enriched discrimination and disadvantage![15]

An HMI report of seven multiethnic comprehensive schools found all schools convinced of the importance of the quality of relationship between the school and the wider community, but reported that their attempts to involve the local community in the life of the school had not met with success. Interestingly, the report comments that those schools where links out into the community have been established found themselves more confident in dealing with issues such as prejudice, discrimination, racial intolerance and *unequal representation* (my italics), but that only two schools had school councils, where pupils freely discussed relationships between the school and the local community. Only four schools had parent-teacher associations, and even in these the activity was largely in the field of fund-raising and social activities![16]

It is perhaps not surprising then that the passage of the 1980 Education Act, laying on schools and Local Education Authorities the statutory duty to publish certain kinds of information for parents, is seen by many as merely a cosmetic exercise![17] Even the very modest statutory requirements published by the Secretary of State the following year had been anaesthetized in passage and remained sometimes unobserved in 1982 due to economic problems![18]

In view of the miserable progress made in home-school cooperation and community-school partnership it was only to be expected that the Rampton Committee might find that

> One of the strangest impressions which we have formed from our visits and discussions has been of the wide gulf in trust and understanding between schools and West Indian parents![19]

In spite of the main theme running throughout the report, the committee apparently found no evidence of lack of interest on the part of parents – sometimes quite the reverse – but it did find that West Indian parents' views and motives were, in some cases, misunderstood, and even disregarded, and the background research volume to the report pointed to the generally low involvement of West Indian parents with their children's schools, indicating that the school itself presented a considerable barrier.[20]

At almost the same moment, the Home Affairs Committee of the House of Commons found that

> Although some authorities apparently made a particular effort to include parent governors from ethnic minority groups, they were conspicuous by their absence in several of the cities visited by the Sub-Committee.[21]

Yet the Committee alluded to the importance of formal structures associated with a school reflecting the community it serves. In other words, the power structure in which the school is set should not solely represent the party political responses of local government but more importantly the composition and cultural make-up of the community which the school is intended to serve. Indeed, in other societies, this demand would appear so reasonable as not to need stating nor arguing as one of the mainstays of legitimacy. Yet in that same summer, as John Rex pointed out,

> ... with our cities burning and the clear demonstration that young blacks among others have no sense of the legitimacy of our institutions as they stand, it (the controversial publication of the abridged Rampton Report) looked like a disaster.[22]

In the light of such a disaster one would have expected an urgent debate about how to establish, sustain and enhance the legitimacy of educational provision and institutions in the minds and hearts of the inner-city and ethnic minority communities. But in spite of the Government taking note of the recommendations of the Scarman Report on the riots, and in spite of minor concessions such as the Secretary of State's decision not to close a multicultural comprehensive school in Liverpool and disperse its mainly black pupils to other schools, 'because of possible educational and social consequences', no such debate had commenced by early 1982.

School community interaction in pursuit of the multicultural curriculum

It remains therefore for us to ask in this chapter what in practice that discourse means which I have argued is an essential part of the effective development of a real multicultural education, and where the nodal points for its development may be identified in the present provision. By discourse is meant a process of human communication, including an accepted equality of the parties concerned, in negotiation and co-decision about real issues of power and access to resources in society. It cannot mean more provision of information by one party to the other, although that exchange will inevitably be a part, but only a part of any meaningful discourse. On the other hand, it does predicate the free availability of information to which either of the parties may have legitimate title. Disputes concerning title would themselves be the subject of discourse, as would the criteria by which discourse could be conducted. But what does that imply in terms of the school and its attempts to provide multicultural education in general and a multicultural curriculum in particular?

Given that multicultural education implies, as I have argued in Chapter One, that many cultures are regarded as legitimate in society and that such an equality has impact on the curricular offerings of an education system and a school, the provision of valued knowledge should to the highest degree possible be a selection from all cultures, although not necessarily equally. Most teachers and educationists, and of course the politicians and administrators whose role is in the field of education, cannot have first hand acquaintance with all cultures represented in society. They will therefore need to engage in dialogue to discover and agree that capital which needs to be valued to the extent that it is included either in the common core of all schools or in the wider enriched curriculum of the school, available differentially to different pupils.

To give an example, contained in a document drawn up by Ealing Community Relations Council: the central core for all pupils would include knowledge of matters such as race and factors pre-disposing to racial and cultural prejudice, whereas the options would include an opportunity for pupils to choose to undertake a detailed study of the land of their forefathers, and of Punjabi, Hindi, Urdu, Hungarian etc. This statement indicates that as a centre of Asian settlement, Ealing would establish itself as a centre for Asian language work. The related point about potent (and viable) participation is well made in the suggestion that the presence of representatives of the various ethnic groups is appropriate – not artificially contrived, but resulting from the participation of those groups in PTA committees, Boards of Governors, etc[23]

This statement, whilst embryonic, does have the 'buds of discourse' viable for further growth. The school is clearly seen as responsible for reflecting the knowledge capital of the local community and even enhancing it. Community involvement is seen as a high priority and such involvement is envisaged as taking place at a potent and influential level. Finally, a distinction is made between what is necessary for all in a multicultural society and what is available for some to choose if they so wish.

A further good example of the interactive dimension of discourse 'around' a curriculum is provided by recent writing by Hargreaves advocating an integrated course in community studies, where the pupils sometimes move out into the community to learn and, on other occasions, outsiders with relevant cultural capital come into the school. Hargreaves argues that as communities become more interdependent, there is a need for members of those communities to foster and further the interests of their own communities without infringing the rights of other individuals or communities. Tellingly he points up the need for improvement in competence in resolving conflicting demands amongst and between those communities.[24]

A further example is the chain of projects which led to the Lambeth Whole School Project, where the initial development work took place against the background of the premise that 'the cultural base of a successful school must be compatible with the cultural base of the community it serves'.[25] Naturally, this cannot exclude a broader compatibility relevant to the future needs of society, the young people themselves in that society and the community's future economic requirements.[26]

Drawing on the community's cultural capital

Local authorities appear to have taken a rich variety of initiatives to draw on the cultural capital of the community whilst at the same time linking it more closely to the school. In some cases, as in the county of Avon, this has taken the form of a centre which has attempted to collect a bank of resources. Considered in conjunction with the Liaison Group established between the Avon Education Department and the Bristol Council for Racial Equality the initiatives constitute important but modest landmarks on the road to greater discourse, based on the recognition of the resource implications for the teacher's professional skill and knowledge capital and the need for meaningful dialogue with the representatives of the local communities.[27] It is interesting, however, to note that in spite of this the Commission for Racial Equality, commenting on the Bristol disturbances, advised *inter alia* that the Local Education Authority should

> encourage greater contacts between the schools and the black community by the use of liaison workers, the creation of parent-teacher organizations, the appointment of ethnic minority parents and local residents as school governors etc[28]

And a further recommendation submitted by an individual referred to

> the prejudiced attitude of teachers in categorizing Black and Asian children, the bias and often degrading curricular and teaching materials... and the apparent lack of commitment to multicultural education, all contributes to racial disadvantage among ethnic minorities.

A good example of the involvement of parents in schools leading to their involvemnt in curriculum development is contained in the evidence of the Leicestershire County Council to the Home Affairs Committee. Home-school liaison is quoted as being the Authority's first priority and three developments are quoted of which one, the 'parents' room' section, may be further cited here. Parental involvement, one Headteacher is quoted as saying, begins in the nurseries. Parents come in each Monday afternoon with their children and discuss such items as dress, food, money, rhymes, pre-reading and pre-number. The mothers teach one of the teachers new songs, new dances and nursery rhymes, discuss different religions and discuss any problems which may have arisen. The liaison with parents is said to lead to involvement with Diwali, and a videotape, for circulation amongst the community, was made of the parents' and children's involvement.[30] The impact of such involvement of the community in the school is traced through into displays of artefacts lent by parents, home corners with saris, Asian cooking utensils, West Indian and Asian recipes, the inclusion of dance, movement and music from all cultures.[31]

Now the importance of this example is not necessarily in the substance, for there is little doubt that many schools in Bradford, Birmingham, Brixton and elsewhere must be involved in similar kinds of curriculum development, but the strategy adopted as an example of the way in which the community's cultural capital may be used to the benefit of pupils, teachers and the broader community. After all the bases of literacy, numeracy and music may remain constant whilst the exemplification of the concepts, principles or rules can take many different forms, and we have known since the time of Herbart that to hook onto something which is familiar can facilitate learning.

A cognate suggestion was made by Craft some time ago when he suggested that value transmission and curriculum presentation ought to be regarded separately. He continues,

> The need to provide relevant and interesting learning structures, using the local and the familiar as a starting point..... Relevance and recognition of the validity of a local subculture as a central teaching technique are quite

compatible with value transmission involving a problem-solving approach in which perseverance over time and the exercise of individual judgement are important features.[32]

What I am arguing for goes beyond but builds upon what Craft is proposing, insofar as it would identify an overall rationale for the separation of values, concepts, skills and modes of inquiry from the content which was the medium for their acquisition into the cognitive biography of the child. For this local community involvement would be indispensable.

A policy statement on Multicultural Education from the Brent Education Authority sees it in this way:

> Essentially what is required is a change in the content of the knowledge system, while retaining the agreed worthwhile concepts, skills and principles of the various subject areas....If the curriculum in the relevant subject areas could be written in a conceptual form, deduced from its present content, meaningful change would be possible.[33]

and later:

> With such a conceptual curriculum it would be possible to teach by reference to exemplars chosen from the multicultural knowledge domain. In that way an educationally sound curriculum could be taught but through a knowledge system of content which will accord respect and dignity and worthwhileness to pupils whatever their reference groups.[34]

What is needed is the rationale and the discourse to 'put it together'.

Some readers may, however, doubt the feasibility of such an exercise, for it is indeed an ambitious enterprise demanding the complete rethinking of the subject matter of the school curriculum, the discarding of its ethnocentric content, and its examination for the underlying skills, attitudes, conceptual development and modes of inquiry which could be used as the grist to the mill of the collaborative reconstruction of a new multicultural curiculum. Some might even doubt that teachers would have the skill.

Fortunately, we have an example of teachers having joined together as a group to attempt just this. Between 1977 and 1980 a group of teachers in the London Borough of Merton, drawn from different levels of the education system, examined the ways in which children of different ages gained an understanding of the concepts and methods of working of history, geography and the social sciences. In Part Three of the document an attempt is made to chart the development of children's learning in social studies, their cognition, attitudes and values and knowledge of the concerns and methods of the disciplines. A final appendix sketches the mapping skills which children should acquire *in the course of their school lives*.[35]

The question thus arises as to whether, if this can be done for social studies, it can also be done for multicultural education. Bearing in mind that the two areas are cognate and that many of the skills, values, methods of approach and inquiry will be the same or similar, there seems no reason to believe that if there were the will, there could not also be the way. Incidentally, such a curriculum would also fulfil one of the major conditions for a multicultural curriculum enunciated in Chapter Three, namely that it should involve as high a level of rational thinking and conceptual development as is conducive with the child's ability: in other words it is not seen as a 'soft option'. For such a curriculum the community's cultural capital is indispensable and for this—or at least to unlock the barriers to such capital—the community will need to be much more directly involved.

Involving the community in the curriculum

It is time again to pick up the thread of our discussion, that discourse which I have argued is necessary for a multicultural curriculum. In doing this I should like to use a concept introduced in a recent publication by Bhikhu Parekh, namely sympathetic imagination, that is, the ability to be able to rise above our own values, preferences and views of the world and to enter into other people's with an open mind. Parekh suggests that, without it, we cannot understand other cultures, societies and historical epochs.[36] And yet, as I have argued in Chapter One and again in Chapter Three, understanding (and knowledge) of other cultures is a necessary prerequisite to that respect for persons and their cultures which is a basic ethic of our multicultural society. As the Schools Council project recognizes,

> The availability of such culturally diverse knowledge will be a necessary rather than a sufficient condition for reaching the goal of respect.[37]

As I understand Bhikhu Parekh's point, sympathetic imagination, as opposed to artistic, creative or aesthetic imagination, has much in common with what Freire calls conscientization: that is, the need for a prospective teacher to identify with the cultural and economic circumstances of the people with whom he wishes to involve himself in a dialogue of learning, to take them on their merits in a process of free interaction which is generative of cultural norms. I have argued elsewhere that this kind of discussion free from domination is a major characteristic of the interdependent curriculum ideology.[38] Such discourse certainly involves a close, mutual, 'educational' involve-ment with and of the community in the curriculum of the school, and it cannot be supplanted by repression through the power of knowledge, or the discourse is destroyed.

To some extent the writing of the German social theorist Habermas is of assistance in helping to identify the distinction which I am making between the involvement of the community in free and balanced dialogue with an educational institution, in which it has a vested interest, and the repression of that dialogue by technical rules supportive of existing power structures. Habermas distinguishes between *purposive-rational action*, governed by technical rules, means-ends relationships and the extension of the power of technical control, and *interaction*, governed by free and mutually accepted consensual norms.[39] To counter the current alienation of large numbers of the school population and their community from educational institutions such as schools, a free-fall 'encounter of a close kind' is necessary, with both parties willing to engage in interaction productive of consensual norms. One school, feeling its way towards the kind of learning community necessary to support interdependent curriculum development based on discourse and a full and potent share by that community in determining how they should be served and could, put it this way:

> ...we recommend that the school takes substantial, urgent but sensitive steps towards ridding itself of being a closed, dominating institution. We have considerable skills, the local community has countless others. For the sake of the children we need to form a professional trusting partnership.[40]

To achieve the kind of interdependent discourse about curriculum and the concomitant involvement of parents and the wider community, a number of different strategies have already been tried, and some of these have already been referred to in this chapter including opportunities for interlearning by parents and teachers. Two issues, however, appear so fundamental to the issue of school-community interdependence as to merit further emphasis; and both are related to the issue of communicative balance.

Firstly, it is unreasonable immediately to expect all local communities to have broadly available the English language resources which would be needed to support such involvement, participation and co-determination as are involved in school-community, interdependent curricularizing. A recent survey, for instance, indicates that roughly one million adults in this country have English as a second language and that so far only a small fraction of these are in ESL classes or home tuition schemes.[41] As numbers of recent writings and reports have indicated this is an area where coordinated action is urgently needed and one which could yield enormous dividends in the increased participation and contribution of the individuals concerned to the life of the nation. More closely related to our theme, it is an essential prerequisite to the movement of ethnic minority members along the continuum of relationship with the formal education of their children, from alienation, through receptive comprehension, involvement and participation to full codetermination.

Secondly, and related to the question of English as a second language, is the issue of mother-tongue teaching and learning. Again a recent survey indicates that most Asian parents would like their children to learn their mother tongue to examination level.[42] Here initial success could easily be achieved by school-home communication (and vice versa) being in mother tongue as well as English, in the provision of interpreting for parents' evenings, and in the use of 'experts' from the community to teach mother tongue in the school where no teacher possesses the expertise. Indeed the area of mother tongue may yet prove to be one of the potentially most fruitful encounters between the traditional and the new, the 'dominant' and the 'minority', across school curriculum, school organization and community development issues.

A recent policy statement of the National Association for Multiracial Education catches some of the spirit of this rich opportunity where it recommends, as measures to be urgently taken:

> ... to ensure that the use of these languages in schools is encouraged and promoted...;
> to involve parents, relatives and friends of minority pupils to the fullest extent in the work of the schools and to provide for communication with them in their respective languages;
> to provide for the teaching of these languages within the normal school curriculum...[43]

One further suggestion of the Policy Statement, for the establishment of the closest possible links with supplementary and/or voluntary schools, seems an important avenue of further school-community cooperation, particularly in view of the favourable review of such schools in Maureen Stone's recent work.[44]

Management practices for pluralism and participation

I have argued in Chapter One that the classroom ethos is interdependent with that of the school. Thus attempts at curriculum reform and new teaching/learning strategies appropriate to multicultural education have to be backed up by perceptive school management which can facilitate both the development of a multicultural curriculum and the initiation of gradual community involvement leading to codetermination.

There is little doubt that many teachers will feel concerned that such open and accountable management may lead to a diminution of their respect and professional status. Equally there is little doubt that the implicit of multicultural education is a change in that status: I would argue, an amelioration, for this reason. The whole trend of our society at the moment is to the greater involvement of citizens in decisions which affect them and their families. As a consequence formerly ascribed status is in decline and is gradually being replaced by that which a person or profession earns. Because it is earned in the full light of public interest, the status achieved by the teacher is more valuable. As a number of writers have pointed out, he is *in* authority rather than *an* authority. In the end his professionalism is more surely founded, more widely recognized and more publicly acclaimed than previously and his influence as a professional is therefore more potent and more broadly felt.

For this broader role, new kinds of management practices and new relationships are essential and it will be up to each school to work these out in conjunction with its community. It could start by asking the kinds of questions suggested in two recent Schools Council Reports, *Multi-ethnic Education* and *The Practical Curriculum*,[45] perhaps above all:

> Has the school made use of its parent body, its local community, its governors and its local education authority as critical friends in helping in its self awareness?[46]

The language is rather purposive-rational, the criterion seems undirectional, but as a start, and after all, there are no people better fitted than friends to tell the professional a few home truths. And it does emphasize the point that often the most obvious resources for multicultural education, the pupil body and the community, are rarely used efficiently. In this connection, a Canadian innovation introduced in response to the rapidly changing cultural context of a school's neighbourhood is worth briefly noting: naming a member of the school staff as a community learning resources consultant, whose task it is to become directly involved with various groups and agencies in the neighbourhood in order to 'beam' those changes back to the school, whilst conversely and at the same time providing information to that community about the school's changing curriculum.[47]

But such initiatives have to be placed in the context of where we wish to go in the management of the multicultural school, and in this respect my own view is that we must seek, however gradually, to move through four phases of community participation in our schools:

1. Firstly, we must move from the efficient provision of information and its collection and collation internally within the school and the wider community to the application of that information to the school, its curriculum and organization, and to the wider community. This implies both the right to information and a willingness for interchange of that information.

2. The second stage would then be one of heightened involvement, through consultation, of parents, pupils and the wider community in decisions affecting them and their own children. To some extent this is a transition and training phase where all parties are involved in rapid interlearning in the pursuit of new knowledge and skills.

3. A third phase is greater participation in all modes of school life by parents and the wider community at all levels and a reciprocal movement by the school into the community. This is the first stage of what I call *active* and *potent* participation and it presupposes and embraces successful completion of the previous stages. It includes the right to both information and a voice, and broader participation in teaching by parents, as in the Haringey Reading Project, which found that active parental help with reading has had a positive effect on the reading performance of children in some multiethnic, inner city primary schools.[47]

4. A fourth phase, building on the other three, is that of codetermination or 'partnership decision-making' with the parents and wider community across the range of issues which are of mutual concern. It implies not just having a right to information or a voice or to influence decisions but to representative codetermination of decisions at different levels – and of course, needless to say, membership on a more than token basis of decision-making bodies.

A random, initial and incomplete list of management practices which have been tried and found of use in the United Kingdom and abroad might well include the following:

1. dissemination of all school information in languages appropriate to the school;

2. involvement of ethnic minority members on governing bodies;

3. parent teacher associations with a strong representation of ethnic minority community members and staff;

4. translation and interpreting service for parents' evenings;
5. use of multilingual signs on school property;
6. pupil councils with strong representation of minority pupils;
7. involvement of bilingual personnel at pre-school, enrolment and guidance levels in the school and in the community;
8. use of appropriate minority languages for communications with the home and wider community;
9. use of school facilities for ethnic community activities including supplementary schools;
10. employment of teachers' aides and other ancillary staff who are bilingual and/or members of minority countries;
11. involvement of parents in reading stories, in minority languages, informal teaching of those languages, providing information and advice on projects, and in conjunction with their guidance, teaching children at home;
12. stocking of school libraries with books and material representative of the school's multicultural community with the advice and participation of that community;
13. school excursions jointly led by ethnic minority parents and teachers to places such as Gurdwaras, which emphasize the cultural diversity of the school;
14. discussion and consideration of ethnic norms of groups when discussing sport and social functions, school meals and assemblies, etc.[49]

A working partnership: learning to share and sharing to learn

The kind of new, more equal relationship which has been suggested above is gradually being introduced in many parts of the United Kingdom by enterprising local authorities, schools and teachers in working partnership with their pupils, parents and wider communities. On the face of it, there is a lot of evidence that, given the right context, lay, professional and administrative members of the education service have been prepared to rethink their educational philosophy and practice in response to new perceptions of the multicultural nature of our society and in pursuit of an appropriate educational provision.

But the kinds of experiments and initiatives which I have referred to do involve substantial change at a time of great insecurity for the teaching profession. Ultimately, a democratic society cannot coerce. It must seek to work through persuasion. Nor would it be prudent to underestimate the forces in society and in education which seek overtly and covertly to resist, even to sabotage, the development of a more pluralist and equitable educational system. We only need remind ourselves of the activities of extreme groups, the refusal of Government to make a clear and unequivocal commitment to the United Kingdom as a multicultural society, remaining discriminatory legislation, the obstinate refusal of certain prestige educational institutions to admit women, and the alleged barring of members of certain ethnic groups from certain prestige regiments in the army, to bring us down to earth and make us realize what a great deal still needs to be done.

There is an urgent and pressing need to agree on a rationale for a philosophy, content, practice and implementation of multicultural education which presupposes a working partnership in pluralism by all groups which wish to move in that direction. Whilst such a rationale cannot be monolithic, neither can it be totally fragmented, or progress will be negated and energy dissipated. Yet a pluralist society demands a pluralism of solutions and the recognition of different levels of partnership within the education system. Thus the recognition of different levels of partnership referred to has to be at local, institutional and intra-institutional levels as well as at national level. Above all it needs to be based on the appreciation that in a pluralist, democratic society the quest for dialogue is a journey which is never finally completed.

The need for and function of research and evaluation

The quest for dialogue is inevitably also a quest for information, for knowledge, for professional and personal renewal and for greater expertise. For this reason, it is inherent within this kind of working partnership, that the role of teacher as researcher brims over into the school and its broader relationships with the community. Rapidly changing cultural backgrounds, where all cultures are lively, adaptive and growing, necessitate a continual process of adaptation on the part of school and staff. Teachers need to know how their community is changing and how the service which they are offering is matching the needs of that community. They need to know how their community appraises them and how their pupils are faring. And so one could continue. But the important thing is that, in the multicultural school, research, or let us call it monitoring, evaluation, self and institutional evaluation, reflexive consideration of living, teaching and learning, can no longer be seen as separate from the activities of the school. They are an integral part of its responsibility to its pupils, its community and itself, although naturally not without tensions.[50]

Thus, whether through ethnographic studies or surveys of opinion, large scale or small, joint or individual, funded or barely floated, each multicultural school will need to begin the process of getting to know itself, its pupils and its community better by dint of that deliberate and systematic act of reflexion, which we call research. There are important resource considerations involved but through partnership the solution of these problems may well be found to be easier. At the very least, I would suggest that each school will need some of the following information:

1. an ethnographic study of the school and its cultural and social context;
2. a monitoring of its own curriculum, including syllabuses, and organization on an ongoing basis;
3. an appraisal of its appointments and staffing policies, both internal deployment and new appointments across the board;
4. a continuing review of its assessment and examinations procedures for their cultural fairness;
5. a mechanism for jointly monitoring the compatibility of its curriculum with its community;
6. a more independent appraisal of its internal functioning;
7. a continuing review of its mechanisms for the involvement of parents and pupils in decision-making;
8. a provision for dialogue with cultural groups and alternative voluntary schools and educational provision;
9. a review of its provision of extra-curricular activities;
10. monitoring of materials, texts and other resources for their racism and cultural prejudice;
11. surveys of staff and pupil attitudes to and opinions on change within the school.

No list is ever complete. It can only be a starting point and no doubt, many teachers can immediately suggest additional items and some will have already done some of the above. Each school will wish to consider its own position carefully. The point remains, however, that multicultural education is by its very nature a reflexive process in which research is an indispensable informant and, in dialogue with the broader community, an eloquent companion.

Summary
This chapter has:

1. summarized briefly the post-war development of parent-teacher, school-community relations;
2. argued the need for school-community interaction in pursuit of the multicultural curriculum;
3. given examples of ways in which schools can draw on the community's cultural capital;

4. offered some instances of community involvement in the curriculum;
5. discussed some management demands of multicultural education;
6. sketched a typology of community involvement in the life of a school;
7. suggested the imperative of a new working partnership at all levels;
8. outlined one or two functions of research as an essential part of multicultural education.

5 Resources for multicultural curriculum development: an introductory overview

The development of a multicultural curriculum along the lines suggested in this book presents massive, but not insuperable, resource problems for the teacher, which are all too often minimized, neglected or even ignored by those who advocate the introduction of multicultural education. But the resource challenge inherent within the multicultural curriculum is first and foremost a challenge to the professionalism and ingenuity of the teacher. For, just as the development of the individual teacher is an indispensable corollary of multicultural education, it will be apparent that the term covers such a huge area of expertise, language and skill, that no person can expect to be able to cover it alone. The range of issues, stretching from the holistic redesign of the curriculum to the changes needed in existing subject areas and the requirement for special provision in mother tongue, bilingualism or English as a second language must presuppose team work and a team approach to the staff development needs which are thrown up by the multicultural curriculum: it presupposes a professional discourse about the support necessary in pursuit of the multicultural curriculum, its preparation, implementation and evaluation.

This chapter therefore begins with a brief assessment of the staff development needs which might be involved in rethinking a school's curriculum along multicultural lines. I then proceed to offer a personal selection of books and materials in some of the major component areas of multicultural education: reference material, the theoretical background, curriculum development in general, particular aspects of curriculum, the language issue, organizations, associations and institutions which may be able to offer assistance.

It is important to emphasize, however, that it is not my intention in this chapter to attempt a comprehensive bibliographical coverage of the fields and to identify all resources for them. Rather it is my aim, having taken note of some of the major issues, to chart the range, indicating nodal points and promising avenues of further growth, some of them as yet slightly off the beaten track. Sometimes I shall be giving sources and exemplifying what is available, even where it may not carry the label 'multicultural,' if I consider that the material might be helpful in the design, development and implementation of the multicultural curriculum. It cannot be stressed too strongly that such an approach inevitably reflects the personal choice and experience of the author and that other writers might have a very different 'bibliographical biography'.

There are a number of reasons for adopting this approach. Firstly, there are already a number of resource books on multicultural education from home and abroad, and the overview prepared by Gillian Klein for the Schools Council, for example, offers an up-to-date and useful starting point for the busy teacher. Secondly, a number of organizations now have considerable experience, and the resource as well, in putting together more comprehensive lists. Some of these are statutory organizations such as the Commission for Racial Equality, some are international in orientation such as the Commonwealth Institute, others are voluntary associations or organizations such as the National Association for Multiracial Education or the Runnymede Trust, and yet others are local authorities such as the Centre for Urban Educational Studies (CUES) in London. In the context of such competition, it is important for the 'home academic' to be realistic about his limitations!

In any case, discussions are already well advanced on the construction of a Resources Information Bank on Multicultural Education at the Schools Council (RIBMESC), whose goal will be to provide a comprehensive data bank on resources relating to multicultural education; the National Association for Multiracial Education put forward a proposal at the Annual Conference in 1981 for a project to devise ways of organizing the often extremely good materials being produced by some local authorities. By April 1982 discussions on the implementation of this proposal through the establishment at Bulmershe College of Higher Education in Reading of a computerized information bank, concerned with resources being produced by local authorities in the field, were already well advanced. So there is already an appreciation of the problem and the promise of some speedy action.

Thirdly, however, a chart indicating some basic sources, including some which might be considered slightly 'off the beaten track' for many British teachers, seemed to be more helpful than a poor recapitulation of what already exists elsewhere. Fourthly, it seemed that such a charting approach was more in line with the charting approach of the rest of the book, than a solely bibliographical listing would be. (A select bibliography is, in any case, appended at the end of this book).

This is essentially a book about the multicultural curriculum and if we were to include the literature on all aspects of both multicultural education and curriculum, the field is so vast and overwhelming that it would be impossible to do bibliographical justice to it, even if the book comprised nothing but lists of books and materials. Decisions concerning the exact resources necessary and available are ultimately for the individual teacher, school and community, albeit often in concert. For, if there is a message in this chapter as in the last, it is not to take the whole burden of staff and resource development on one pair of shoulders, professional or not.

Human resource considerations

But if the introduction of a multicultural curriculum confronts the teacher with resource and retraining problems of such magnitude that no individual can hope to solve all of them alone, it also offers the teacher great opportunities for personal and professional growth and satisfaction as well. It is important, for example, that the resource which is nearest to the teacher and so obvious that it may be ignored is not neglected; namely the teacher's pupils, colleagues and the community. Through learning from his/her pupils, by means of collaborative learning strategies and collegial team work, through lay-professional interdependence between teachers and pupils and teachers and the community, there are huge untapped resources which become available. The corollary of that appreciation and exploitation of community resources is inevitably a fundamental but not unprecedented change in the role of the teacher from that of 'keeper of the word-hoard' to that of 'editor and sometimes author of new knowledge': the critical and evaluative role referred to earlier on several occasions.

It is not an exaggeration to say that the teacher will be encountering new connections between knowledge yielded by many sources, and new relationships between values and persons which have not been 'pieced together' previously, perhaps not even existed previously. But in order to capitalize on the rich resource sitting in front of them, teachers will need to get to know their pupils in greater detail as individuals and as members of various communities which will need encouragement to contribute to the available knowledge and resource pool. It is in this sense that the 'open classroom' advocated earlier becomes not only a necessity for the transmission of knowledge—a traditional function of teachers—but also for the newer knowledge and resource production role of the teacher, 'editor and author'. The relationships demanded by that new role are the combination whereby the 'community and pupil treasure chests' of resource can be released. They are the means whereby the critical-cultural scanning and garnering role of the school can be fulfilled through the semi-permeable membrane of the criteria referred to previously, based on the societal ethic and social imperatives.

Pupils are great cultural healers and encouragement to them to bring artefacts and books to school (as well as their cultures), to translate where they have the competence to do so, to take lead roles in developing projects concerning particular festivals, customs, handicrafts, music, cookery and the history and geography of other countries, perhaps their parents' homeland, will surely be richly reflected in improved relationships with the wider community. It is in this sense that the pupils may be seen to fulfil the role of 'cultural go-between' in relation to parents and teachers, pupils and teachers, pupils and pupils and the community and the school.

Then too, 'majority' pupils and staff may learn by seeing minority pupils in non-classroom roles. Playing such roles may help ethnic minority pupils to develop, maintain and extend a legitimate pride in their (and our) cultural heritage and, at the same time, enable majority staff and pupils to update their knowledge of the culture of various groups and the contribution they have made to the development of their own country and others abroad. To this end, various formal and informal channels are available in addition to classroom roles, namely clubs, exhibitions and other extracurricular activities which can be important seed-beds for the generation of new knowledge and resources. By extension too, and as pointed out in Chapter Four, strong links with the supplementary or voluntary schools are also a good means of achieving additional cultural resources, whilst at the same time strengthening community 'connections' and channels of communication. Sometimes through such means a teacher is born, and a chasm bridged.

Staff development considerations

But staff not only need to capitalize on such pupil and community resources, they also need to seek interest in each other's capital and provide for the easy exchange of information, ideas and sources to which they may individually have access. Often this is done informally in the marketplace of the staff-room or the informality of the corridor, but some schools have found additional rather more formalized means to be necessary, such as a regular item on the staff meeting agenda on resources and resource development, a special exchange notice board for 'trading' of resource information, or the designation of a member of staff with particular responsibility for obtaining and disseminating information and resources and keeping up-to-date with what is available. A lot depends, of course, on the size of staff and the style of the school.

On occasions, this task of masterminding the school's cultural resource collection is located with the librarian. In other cases, it is another member of staff, or in some authorities it is envisaged as being part of the supra-institutional role of the advisory staff or, as in the Inner London Education Authority, a team of advisers. Several local authorities, usually in the van of responding to the resource needs inherent in multicultural education for the population which they serve, have set up specialized consultative collections, sometimes including both reference and loan facilities. Perhaps one of the most advanced of these is the ILEA's Centre for Learning Resources, although all are modest indeed in comparison with the need and the provision in some overseas countries such as the United States.

Whatever 'style' the authority and school adopt, it is important to make sure that the responsibility and the opportunity are seen as collegial. For, just as the individual member of staff will need to identify for him or herself a profile of professional development, so the school will need to draw up a flexible policy for staff development as a whole which can sustain the diverse demands which 'going multicultural' makes. The human resource of the school is its most valuable asset and both collegially and individually staff need to look to their needs. Workshops, do-it-yourself groups, school-based conferences and meetings within the school or on a joint basis with neighbouring schools or groups of teachers can be very rewarding. Sometimes a local college, polytechnic or university may provide a tutor or small in-service fund. Some local authorities too provide special small funding in the field[3] and the Schools Council programmes of work favour teacher groups and joint initiatives as does the Morrell fund. Looking wider afield, application could be made to support a member of staff to go abroad under some such scheme as the Central Bureau for Educational Visits and Exchanges, or the Intensive Study Visit Scheme.

Members of the local community are often delighted to be invited in to talk to staff – and even teach them – about their community, its customs, songs, dances, etc. Sensitivity is needed to avoid any hint of unpaid exploitation – it can be a contentious issue – but mostly normal human social courtesy is sufficient to dispel doubts about motives. Visits to local mosques, temples and community groups and projects, to local ethnic minority businesses, clubs and cafes can yield invaluable learning and insights on how to push back the frontiers of a formerly ethnocentric curriculum. Some schools have set up working parties to advise them on what such action they should take and how, but whatever strategy is adopted, if the gain is to be maximized, it needs to be accompanied by a system of feedback and sharing information.

Indeed information dissemination is identified by a recent research report as being one of the major issues in the present provision of in-service education in the field. Not only does it comment that the communication network in schools is spasmodic[4] but it also draws attention to the need for schools to find more effective ways of 'debriefing' their colleagues who have been on in-service courses[5]

Many staff wish and need to attend courses and conferences and, in the present financial circumstances, the school as a whole needs to make sure that it can gain full benefit from such attendance. Local courses are provided in teachers' centres, in colleges, in polytechnics and in universities, by organizations such as the local or National Association for Multiracial Education, the National Union of Teachers, the Commission for Racial Equality either directly or through its teacher education Advisory Committee or its working parties. Lists of short and long courses are issued by the Department of Education and Science and analogue departments responsible for education in other parts of the country. Publicity is sent to all schools.

Increasingly too, institutions of higher education offer an opportunity for teachers to do a project or dissertation, as part of a diploma, part-time B.Ed., higher degree or research degree, on their own school and its needs. Case study approaches and individual and institutional evaluation studies are slowly becoming more widespread as such institutions try to respond more closely to the needs of schools and the profession. Clearly, professional safeguards are necessary in some of this work and these are gradually emerging as a greater partnership grows between schools and colleges in response to both evaluation and 'teacher as researcher' movements as well as a clearer recognition of professional interdependence in a time of growing financial stringency and educational contraction.

At a national level institutions such as the Centre for Information on Language Teaching, the Society for Research into Higher Education and the Teacher Education Study Group, and organizations such as the National Union of Teachers and the National Association of Teachers in Further and Higher Education have published policy statements and helpful booklets, arranged courses, meetings and conferences where important resource hints can be collected. Centres too, such as the Centre for Multicultural Education at the University of London, the International Centre for Multicultural Education in Birmingham and the Centre at Bradford College provide information, advice and support in and outside their immediate areas. Book exhibitions are organized by teachers' (and headteachers') associations, and publishers and materials production firms set up exhibitions and have representatives visit schools.

Wherever a member of staff attends such a function there should be a system of reporting back if at all possible including, as appropriate, suggestions for further action. A noticeboard concerned exclusively with staff development can help in this respect as can the availability of a short proforma, a display of materials collected, perhaps at lunchtime in the staffroom. Where school staff or parties may have been to the Caribbean or Indian subcontinent, for instance, it is important that the whole school should benefit from the experience and pictures, slides and films can often attract parents into the schools who might not otherwise become involved.

Spurred on by the demands implicit and explicit within the DES 'School Curriculum' document and in Circular 6/81, as also by the new regulations arising from the 1980 Education Act and the need to send out more detailed information to parents (some schools already do this in several languages), some school staffs have discussed and agreed a staff development policy which makes manifest and coherent their commitments to multicultural education. Certainly, where staff sit down together and set out their aims and philosophy, give account of such procedures as those for examination and entry and reflect on the multiculturalism of their provision, it is inevitable that they will begin to share out their knowledge and understandings, and come to appreciate the whole pool of expertise and skill which the staff possess and how this relates to their own. From learning and learning to learn comes learning to improve.

Library provision

Where a major role for the collection and collation of resources falls to one person, such as the 'librarian', it will be apparent that that person is going to need the assistance of colleagues and/or pupils and members of the wider community. The inclusion of fiction, for instance, portraying the history, customs and attitudes of members of different cultural groups in our society, will need to be scrutinized for its balance and lack of bias, racism and prejudice. Does this task necessitate an advisory group? Should it be all professional? Or should pupils and members of the wider community participate? Does material in ethnic languages present particular issues soluble only in the context of community assistance?

Often it is not just a problem of language, but of balance, professionalism, content and appropriateness to the needs and lives of pupils growing up in the United Kingdom of the 1980s. In response to a number of dilemmas and as a practical means of tackling such needs, some schools have adopted a system whereby the title page of foreign language material is translated for the teacher or librarian; this is then put on a sticker on the book and a duplicate is transferred to the catalogue card, with material in different scripts and alphabets being categorized under the next nearest English equivalent. Then, of course, the decision has to be made, whether 'ethnic materials' should be interfiled – which sometimes makes them difficult to find for the very pupils who are most likely to want to seek them out – or whether, on the other hand, they should be shelved in separate cultural groupings, which may seem to emphasize their strangeness.

In times of shrinking capitation allowances, unpalatable decisions about priority allocation of resource have to be made and are often best taken on a collegial, sometimes even on a community, basis. Where this latter happens, it may be that members of ethnic minority communities, whilst not conceding the principle that such material should be provided by the local authority, will be willing to give or lend books, materials and cultural artefacts for exhibition, especially where, having been associated with decisions, they realize that such material may not otherwise be available.

The dispersion of ethnic minority groups and pupils, the range of age and ability, the languages spoken (some may be dialects, or Anglicized versions, or spoken only and not read or written by the persons concerned), of scripts, all accentuate the problem of resources. In another sense, of course, they enrich it. But storage can be a problem as well and decisions have to be taken about the type of material to be included. There will, for instance, be certain core books which all schools will need to possess, even where there are very few or even no ethnic minority pupils: some will be teachers' books such as bibliographies or handbooks or reference texts, including the free and other material from the CRE; others may be monolingual or bilingual dictionaries or books for pupils of a particular age-range or to cover a number of age-ranges. Some will be non-print materials such as records, cassettes and tapes of folk music, songs, stories, plays, etc; slides, posters, filmstrips, films of school journeys or other events, videotapes, of BBC or ITV programmes or historical and local events, the geography of other countries, festivals in local temples; kits, actual costumes, examples of pupils' work, and many other kinds of cultural artefact and handicraft. How, and for how long, should they be stored, catalogued and displayed?

Collegial decisions need to be made as to whether a rigid spatial or catalogue distinction should be made between teachers' books and pupils' books, what criteria should be used in purchasing and selecting and whether all the material is best placed in the library or elsewhere. The questions of additional assistance to the librarian, opening hours for borrowing, possible community and parental involvement will need to be answered, and guidelines may need to be agreed by all staff concerning the main profile of development for the multicultural library.

All the issues raised so far in this chapter are legitimate ones for staff decision and, as appropriate, staff development. They all offer a chance for collegiality, for the recognition of pupil expertise in fields perhaps not possessed by staff and also copious opportunity for closer and more meaningful involvement of ethnic minority communities in the affairs of the school. They could also afford fruitful means of promoting better home-school and school-community relations across the board.

For their part teachers will need to reflect on their priorities, the criteria against which they judge the suitability of material and the public threshold for discussion of such matters. Each school will have a different cultural and resource context, different strengths and different needs, different pupils, communities and staff. It is right that the decisions should best be located there.

In the first part of this chapter I have set out one or two considerations concerning the way in which schools will need deliberately and systematically to set out to achieve a staff and resource development policy if they are optimally to support the introduction of a multicultural curriculum in their school. Whilst emphasizing the distinctiveness of each school and therefore *its* decisions, I have tried to suggest that the staff development and resource development policies pursued will print their distinctive mark on the kind of multicultural curriculum possible. In brief, I have proposed that:

1. staff development must be seen as an integral part of the introduction of a multicultural curriculum;
2. a necessary starting point is an appreciation of the massive staff, pupil and community resource available and its sensitive appraisal and professional exploitation;
3. in capitalizing on pupil and community resource, additional dividends such as improved relationships inevitably accrue;

4. there is a need to identify both institutional and individual staff development profiles;
5. self-help and other opportunities for in-service training of staff should be maximized and there should be proper arrangements for feedback and dissemination;
6. important and explicit decisions need to be taken about library and resource collation policies;
7. collegial and interdependent decisions are appropriate and functional across most of the issues of human and other resource and staff development which the multicultural curriculum implies.

In the rest of this chapter, I intend to suggest one or two resources and sources of information which represent starting points for the teacher and offer a springboard into the literature and resources.

Teacher reference sources

Many teachers have already done a great deal, some of them making highly innovatory contributions to the field, but for some the problem still remains of how to get started. And when you are a neophyte in any area, it is easy to be overwhelmed. This chapter therefore restricts itself to a very few books, materials and sources which seem to be indispensable, plus one or two 'unusual sources'. Inevitably others would make a different selection.

The first step in any case is to get to know your sources and here Gillian Klein's Schools Council publication on resources is the best starting point, containing annotated references on context, teaching, bibliographies and reading for pleasure, and listing organizations, projects, local authority support and the proposed Resources Information Bank on Multicultural Education at the Schools Council. This latter does not include American material which can be obtained through the Educational Research Information Centre (ERIC), via local and educational libraries, the NFER or the International Centre for Multicultural Education at Birmingham, or through the National Clearinghouse on Bilingual Education in Rosslyn, Virginia[7] or the Ethnic Heritage Clearing House in Boulder, Colorado[8] As far as Australia is concerned a useful review of multicultural and migrant education was produced in September 1980 by the then newly established Australian Institute of Multicultural Affairs[9] and two starter 'bibliographies' have been produced by the Education Departments of Tasmania and South Australia[10]

Additionally many local libraries such as those in Brent, Bradford and Birmingham offer valuable services to the teacher, which in some cases include material available for loan. Some of them put together bibliographies of resources or of children's books, for instance, which often reflect the local cultural scene more accurately than national ones can. Individuals too have assembled bibliographies and lists of resources for teachers, sometimes at the ends of books, sometimes as integral parts of a handbook. The early survey by Taylor is still worth looking at and the CRE *World Religions Handbook* contains over 200 pages of reading lists, which in spite of some marked limitations provide a useful beginning.[11] Alternative orientations are provided by the Runnymede Trust and Hicks,[12] with a focus on minorities, and Lynch, on the contribution of different cultural groups to teaching and curriculum.[13] The report of the Schools Council Research Project also has copious references for the 5-13 age range and some of more general applicability across areas like objectives, thematic and early reading work, fantasy and fiction, and a very extensive and useful bibliography for children in this age group.[14] Judith Elkin's book has a practical slant towards the classroom[15] whilst on the other hand the review of research, *Children of West Indian background,* is probably the best example of compilation of research which we possess in the United Kingdom in one subfield at the moment.[16]

The Commission for Racial Equality produces masses of material, much of it free of charge. To mention just one or two items, there is a much revised bibliography for teachers, a list of audio-visual aids, a project on race relations, and reprints from *Education and Community Relations* on such issues as teaching in the multicultural primary school and race in the curriculum.[17] Each usually contains a list of selected CRE publications, including free ones, and periodicals. CRE also issues resource guides and lists of bookshops, ethnic minority organizations and other useful contacts. Membership of voluntary organizations such as The National Association for Multiracial Education, the Children's Rights Workshop and the National Committee on Racism in Children's Books with their respective journals *Multiracial Education, Children's Book Bulletin* and *Dragon's Teeth* also gives access to a wealth of ideas, references, opinions and meetings.[18] Occasional specialized listings and papers, including an early one on criteria for selection of material quoted in Chapter Four, are also available from the Centre for Urban Educational Studies.[19]

The Schools Council has produced some excellent material, which has a good practical tendency and is easily readable and helpful to teachers. The leaflet produced in March 1982 gives a very good overview of current and future funded work, selected publications and initial guidelines on curriculum resources and assessment.[20]

Although details are included within the pamphlet, special reference should be made to the reports which emanated from the controversial and major project in the field in the 1970s.[21]

The thing to remember with the Schools Council is that the output is so rich and the fields covered so diverse that often, even though it does not carry the label multicultural, the material lends itself to use by teachers wishing to roll back the ethnocentrism of their curriculum. The Communication and Social Skills Project[22] is a good example, with some very worthwhile material for the 'pillaging multiculturalist', as of course is material associated with the Humanities Curriculum Project, referred to extensively earlier in this book and probably most easily available directly from the Centre for Applied Research in Education at the University of East Anglia, which is the United Kingdom Centre for training and support of the Bruner material *Man a Course of Study* (MACOS), and where there is a Humanities Project Archive which is available for consultation by teachers.[23]

Similarly teachers will wish to be on the lookout for material from other 'non-multicultural' sources which can be of use. The publications of the Department of Education and Science Further Education Research and Development Unit have contained some excellent curriculum material which lends itself very easily to adaptation for the secondary school.[24] Publishers, too, often produce teaching notes for their material which some may disdain but which can be very supportive, and are often helpfully structured for a teacher seeking the confidence to begin to extend expertise.[25]

The theoretical background

A good initial overview of the theoretical work in the field in the United Kingdom can be obtained through the Open University Reader[26] whilst with certain limitations Morrish's book is still worth selective reference.[27] For the statistical background, useful both to teacher knowledge and teaching purposes, the Runnymede Trust/ Radical Statistics Race Group is a good beginning[28] and the Office of Population Censuses and Statistics occasional papers can be useful.[29]

There are a number of contributions to the theoretical and background curricular literature in this field which should be mentioned. From Australia two books by Bullivant[30] and from the United States a new book by that prolific writer in the field, Banks, and a second edition of one of his earlier ones[31] are helpful in exposing some of the underlying issues, in identifying curricula and curriculum strategies and in helping to render otherwise taken-for-granted presuppositions as problematic. All contain useful bibliographies and are sometimes able to suggest new and neglected potential for work, ideas and resources in multicultural education in this country. From Canada the select bibliography by Mallea and Shea[32] gives a useful point of departure and an earlier resource list identifies material available for classroom use.[33] Clearly teachers will wish to give particular scrutiny to materials from abroad but, wisely used, there is much that we can learn from them.

Back in the United Kingdom, and in the field of books on the curriculum, Stenhouse's two books will be indispensable to any serious student;[34] while teachers will also wish to look at Skilbeck's work and particularly his situational analysis approach to curriculum construction.[35] Lawton's more recent publications offer superb, succinct resumés of fields such as the political background and teaching and learning.[36] On the newer evaluation and accountability dimensions teachers may refer initially to the Schools Council Research study edited by Tawney;[37] the book by Hamilton;[38] the Schools Council evaluation notes[39] and, to emphasize the importance of the teacher-practitioner's considered judgement, Elliott and MacDonald.[40]

Particular issues

In the field of teacher education, a first-class commentary on the current situation, how we arrived there and checklists for action are contained in Craft's book;[41] while for those colleagues interested in the inadequacies of INSET, they may wish to refer to the summary of a recent research project in the field by Eggleston and colleagues at the University of Keele and funded by the DES.[42] Older material from the former Community Relations Commission, the Commission for Racial Equality and the National Association of Teachers in Colleges of Further and Higher Education remains remarkably topical and relevant to the current situation and needs.[43] The series of publications from the American Association of Colleges for Teacher Education is a timely reminder of the kind of material we could be producing.[44]

Several local authorities have issued policy statements, and guidelines have now appeared at both school and authority levels. To cite just two, the Brent Policy Statement[45] and the ILEA guidelines[46] are worth referring to, and the best known school document is probably the Birley High School one.[47]

On issues of race and ethnic minorities, Rose's landmark study of race relations is still worth looking at, as is also Milner's study, based on research evidence from Britain and America, of the ways in which discrimination develops and its effects on black children[48] and the

Scarman Report[49] provides a reminder of what happens when we get it wrong. The Home Office Research Study published in 1981[50] gives a more longitudinal view of ethnic minorities and their development than is usually taken and the Policy Studies Institute is to conduct a further such survey in 1982[51] Still in the field of official but nonetheless critical reports the four volumes of the Parliamentary Select Committee's Report, published in mid-1981[52] are a mine of information, some of it directly relevant to the kinds of initiatives, a few of which have been suggested in this book. In this respect the appendices and evidence in Volumes II to IV are probably the most useful. The Government's response to the report makes interesting, if in some respects gloomy reading[53] There is a brief and most helpful NUT pamphlet on the heredity versus environment debate[54] while Flynn's book gives a more extensive though nonetheless balanced assessment of the scientific evidence[55] Jeffcoate's very readable *Positive Image* has become something of a classic and sets the issues firmly in a classroom and relationship context[56] On the legal background the book by Lester and Bindman is heavy going but is good for the historical development of the issues, which is sometimes forgotten[57]

Some of the early pioneer studies calling for the need for multicultural education indicated the very different social and educational backgrounds with which immigrant children arrived in the United Kingdom[58] Early surveys which looked at arrangements in schools and local authorities with immigrant pupils, conducted by Townsend and Brittan, offer a benchmark from which to plot how far we have progressed in a decade[59] The work and reports of the Select Committee on Race Relations and Immigration concern multiethnic education and latterly the educational needs of children of West Indian origin[60] But the most recent overview is that afforded by the Schools Council survey, which reviewed the work of LEAs and schools in England and Wales, published in summary form in 1981. This stated significantly:

> ...many of those responsible for and involved in multiethnic education...now believe that the presence of minority ethnic group children has implications which go beyond the need for special arrangements and special provision and involve the curriculum generally. Curriculum development...is seen...more as involving a reappraisal of the curriculum as a whole to make it relevant...to all pupils[61]

Its recommendations are set out in a series of action statements, for example for local authorities, for schools, for parents, for community groups and others. It is thus an important first port of call for teacher mariners stocking up for the long journey into multicultural waters.

On guidelines for teachers regarding racial stereotyping the NUT pamphlet is brief and to the point and contains an intial booklist[62] while Whitehead's research indicates the sediment of values and attitudes which an author's views, values and attitudes leave behind and emphasizes the need to scrutinize the material which is used in schools[63] Searle's work in collecting and publishing the prose and poetry of black children and collating the writings of secondary pupils in the East End of London is valuable in itself but also because of the interspersed commentaries about teaching strategies[64]

Language concerns

The area of language in multicultural education is a very broad one with far reaching implications for the whole curriculum, but basically there are two main issues concerned with the learning of English as a second language and mother tongue or mother dialect maintenance. Guidance on the teaching of English as a second language is contained in the book by Derrick[65] while Garvie's work offers practical advice, particularly to teachers of English as a second language to young children[66] For those teachers who are likely to be teaching non-standard English speakers Edwards's work is an indispensible baseline[67] and for those looking for practical advice the work of Barnes and Todd is to be recommended[68] as is that of Tough for the fostering of communications skills in general in the nursery and infant school[69] There are some useful CRE publications including one on language which includes extensive sources such as bibliographies, professional associations and addresses[70] The one on story-telling in second language teaching is very practical and includes some good hints on material and techniques[71]

There is rather less in this country on mother-tongue and such issues as cognitive styles associated with bilingualism and bidialectism. A number of projects have now been commenced, or in two cases completed and results should be available soon in print[72] There is an interesting and provocative article by one of the Directors of the Bradford project[73] and we also have the results of research into the attitudes of various groups to mother tongue teaching[74] At the other end of the spectrum is a very detailed summary of the literature on the effectiveness of bilingual education, from the United States Department of Education[75]

Organizations, associations and institutions

There are now so many organizations, associations and institutions involved in multicultural education that it is only possible to briefly mention a few here. In doing so I shall try to indicate 'kinds' rather than seek to provide any sort of comprehensive coverage. Without doubt, we are very fortunate in having a national association in this field where other multiculturally more mature communities do not. The National Association for Multiracial Education, both nationally and through its local branches, is a veritable powerhouse in the production and exchange of information and its resources. Its national conferences are the 'exchange and mart' of the multicultural field. Other voluntary organizations in the field are ALTARF (All London Teachers Against Racism and Fascism)[76] NATESLA (National Association for the Teaching of English as a Second Language)[77] AFFOR (All Faiths for One Race)[78] and the Minority Rights Groups[79]

Organizations with an international brief which provide information, resources and conferences/seminars include the Commonwealth Institute[80] which also has a library, reference and loan service and a special folder on how to borrow materials. The Embassies and High Commissions of overseas countries often have materials available for loan as well[81] and of course some of the Commission for Racial Equality and Schools Council material mentioned above is a valuable starting point.

Resource Centres are mushrooming now and teachers may like to start by writing for the ILEA Learning Materials Service[82] Catalogues or by contacting the Centre for Urban Education Studies quoted earlier or, for more specialized resources, centres such as the Afro-Caribbean Education Resource Project[83]

Several academic institutions such as universities and polytechnics have now established specialized centres. The one at Birmingham Polytechnic is developing an international repository of resources[84] The Centre for Information on Language Teaching (CILT)[85] provides useful guidance to its field, including English as a second language, as does the Institute of Race Relations (IRR) on race relations and minority affairs[86] In the broader field of development education there is a centre in London where a start can be made[87] and the same applies to the one for Peace Studies in Lancaster[88] Finally, in this brief and initial list, the National Extension College[89] and the Runnymede Trust[90] provide valuable if different services.

In this chapter we have done no more than provide a few nodal points for the teacher so that he or she can begin. Each of the sources mentioned can suggest further areas of resource provision as required by the individual teacher. In the final chapter we look at some of the tasks involved in that process of beginning.

Summary

This chapter has:

1. raised a number of issues concerned with resource and staff development;
2. suggested the need to regard pupils, staff and community as the most important resource available to the school;
3. proposed a number of specific measures for staff development, resource collection and collation and information dissemination;
4. pointed to a small number of sources of information and resource, each of which could be used as a stepping-stone to further information and resources on the multicultural curriculum;
5. referred briefly to a small number of organizations, associations and institutions where teachers could begin their search.

6 The multicultural curriculum: some guidelines for action

To implement the covenant inherent within the kind of multicultural curriculum suggested in this book will be no easy matter. For one thing it would be naive to assume that a majority of the population of this country, let alone its governmental circles and administration, is convinced that Britain in the 1980s is, or should be, a multicultural society. For another, it is unlikely that substantial additional resources will be immediately available for the re-jigging of the professional and cultural capital of the teaching force, which is by and large a necessary accompaniment.

On the other hand teachers in many different parts of the country have demonstrated already that they are the ones who are capable of designing and introducing multicultural curricula and materials. In this respect, it is the grassroots development towards multicultural education which has been most impressive in this country. For this reason, without assuming that all teachers are at the same stage of 'multicultural competence' or that all schools have the same need, this chapter seeks to indicate some initial guidelines for action. I am conscious in doing this that for some teachers a number of the guidelines may already have been implemented but for others I hope that they may be novel in large part.

This chapter takes a look at what needs to be done to strive towards the ideal of a multicultural curriculum at three different levels: the systemic, by which I mean national or local authority level; the institutional, that is the school level; and the individual teacher level.

Some tasks for systemic action: national
Firstly, it is important at the national level that an unequivocal and explicit commitment is made by the government of the day to multiculturalism as one of the basic values of our society. That means not only that there would be legislation, as there is, which outlaws racial discrimination, but that it would cover the whole range of cultural criteria seen as legitimate dimensions of the cultural diversity

of our society. Any remaining discriminatory legislation against particular groups for historical or other reasons should be rescinded. Any loopholes to prejudice or discrimination must be closed so that it is not possible for a particular institution to hide behind charitable status, for instance to discriminate against women, as certain prestigious educational foundations appear to be doing. Nor would it be possible for particular occupational groupings to achieve discrimination *de facto*, whilst of course abhorring it *de lege*, as is alleged to be happening in certain sections of the armed forces.

Additionally, and in the education sector, each of the government departments with responsibility should issue a 'consultative document' on multicultural education which would eventually, after considerable discussion, result in an amended 'School Curriculum' document. This document must acknowledge multiculturalism as something more than an issue, namely, a central and pivotal value domain of our society. As has happened with Circular 6/81 this would need to be followed up by a system of monitoring and evaluation. A revised circular would be necessary and a unit specifically devoted to the appraisal on a national basis of local authorities' and schools' progress towards multicultural education and a multicultural curriculum. The unit would have no inspectorial or enforcement power, but would have the task of providing the information, on the basis of which the normal channels of inspection and enforcement could be set in motion if necessary.

It is important here to note that any talk of coercion is entirely out of place. The process has to be seen as part of that wider process of discourse and dialogue outlined in Chapter Four. As part of its function, however, it is to be hoped that the unit could stimulate professional performance; identify more closely areas of special need; indicate 'good practice' such as collaborative and other learning/teaching strategies, which takes advantage of the cultural diversity of society and the school system; indicate to authorities and schools how they may design and implement their own ongoing review procedures; and assist in the generation of a climate of discussion and dialogue, both lay and professional, which will assist in the involvement of diverse cultural groups in education, its process, organization and control, and the improvement of provision.

Some local priorities for action

Within the context of an overall governmental policy for multicultural education, the partnership between central and local government, by now a traditional strength of education in this country, must continue and be strengthened. Because of the aimlessness of much that passes for multicultural education at the moment, however, all local education authorities will need to formulate, through an exhaustive process of consultation, an approved, explicit and readily understandable policy statement on multicultural education. This might include references to the nature of multiculturalism both nationally and locally, indicating both areas of special need and special provision and those areas which are common to the support of cultural diversity. It will need to include reference to support and resource issues; to be convincing to local minority committees, it is essential that it should include reference to the even-handedness of the systems of education and their examination and pupil appraisal procedures. Such documents will need to be both persuasive and sensitive statements of reason and policy; brief and concise yet comprehensive, societal yet adaptive and expressive of local circumstances, working papers yet firm enought to be susceptible to implementation.

Such an overall policy statement would no doubt include items such as the following. It is the policy of the local education authority:

1. not to discriminate on the basis of race, ethnicity, sex, marital status, disability etc;
2. that the curriculum, teaching methods, material and texts will reflect the cultural diversity of British society, nationally and locally;
3. that one major aim of education and the curriculum will be a reduction in stereotyping and the elimination of prejudice, discrimination and bias;
4. that education will foster appreciation of the unity of human kind and respect for its diversity;
5. that examinations will be 'culture-fair' and even-handed;
6. that teachers will be supported in the achievement of a multicultural education provision appropriate to both local and national needs;
7. to support the maintenance and enhancement of bilingualism in general and mother tongue competence, both oral and written, in particular;
8. to explicitly support equal job opportunities linked with an appreciation of the importance of the recruitment of ethnic minority staff!

Local provision will of course be organized around the focus of local needs, with the need for frequent local 'need-assessment' surveys as a baseline to the response to the differing district, age and cultural profiles. Regular and thorough research and evaluation is an inevitable part of such a policy as are also intensive contacts with the local community and particularly parents. Moreover, if scarce resources are going to be maximally exploited this will call for a networking of resources and the encouragement of a policy of staff exchanges between schools and between education and teacher education.

Within the context of the overall policy statement, distributed to all within the locality, there will need to be operational guidelines which can be drawn up by working parties including officers, advisers, teachers, elected members, community members, parents and, as appropriate, pupils, whose task would be to set out the main parameters for the achievement of the policy statement. It will be necessary, but not sufficient alone, that elected members should participate. Nor is it prudent to envisage the process as a once-and-for-all mechanism but rather part of the continuing discourse, which includes the identification and ordering of priorities for a given financial period and the establishment of an outline schedule of consultation and implementation.

Further, the working parties will need to continually address new areas of knowledge, as the educational implications of adapting policies of multiculturalism deepen and the requirement arises for new policy statements for newly or differently perceived areas of need. The working parties will need, for example, to give attention to the improvement of communications between local authorities, teachers, parents, pupils, minority groups and the community in general, which by dint of its very success may generate new needs and approaches as the intercommunicative competence and intercultural understanding and skills of the parties improve[2].

But the support for teachers and their profession is in many cases totally lacking at the moment, as two recent surveys indicate. At local level a means of stimulating the development of multicultural curricula has to be found through support and in-service provision for teachers. We already know, for instance, that in 1981 at least 18 of the 97 local education authorities surveyed by Matthews were providing special funding for multicultural curriculum development[3] and this seems a practice which has also proved effective in the United States and Australia. But we also know from the same survey that only 14 of the 67 local authorities from whom information was collected referred to links with ethnic minority groups in the community, and that 16 authorities made no provision for in-service education in the field[4]. So there is considerable scope for expansion there.

Equally, the survey by Eggleston and his colleagues indicated the fragmentary and incomplete nature of current INSET provision[5].

There were no methods to ensure help for teachers facing acute difficulty in multicultural classrooms and what help was available was spasmodic and frequently unkown to teachers. Moreover, it was often not related to the needs of schools and minority groups.[6]

Thus, once again, the crucial importance of a coherent and well-supported district-wide policy for the design and implementation of support and in-service provision for teachers is one of the tasks which local authorities will need to attend to urgently, in so far as they have not done so already, and if they wish to develop multicultural provision and multiculturalism. Such support is an essential stepping-stone to the multicultural curriculum and as such it needs to be included in the overall implementation strategy and guidelines. Thus a rolling programme of policy guideline development, implementation, appraisal and improvement will be necessary. From learning to learn and to share will come learning to improve which, in turn, will generate new needs to learn to learn.

I suppose what I am proposing is similar to the process of delivering people from intellectual, moral and spiritual bondage which education represents for many at the moment, and of recognizing education, as Stenhouse argues, as the potential instrument of a redistribution of the means of autonomy and judgement.[7] The right to judgement is redistributed as is the autonomy to feel in a position to formulate tentative judgements subject to critical public appraisal.

The institutional level: some suggestions for beginning

The first task for any school in attempting to plan the introduction of a multicultural curriculum is inevitably a reappraisal of where it has got to, what it offers, with what kind of success and how this reflects and relates to its immediate communities. This is inevitably going to involve a lot of work and for this reason, and for others equally, the task will need to be tackled on a basis of team work. The school is not alone however, and can, if it wishes, have access to pupil and community resources which can greatly share and therefore lighten the burden.

One approach which has been suggested by Reynolds and Skilbeck is that of what they term 'situational analysis'.[8] This involves a review of broader contextual issues (external factors) and the immediate school environment (internal factors). In this first case, this involves such items as community assumptions and values, expectations and requirements of parents and employers and shifts in general ideological movements in society. Amongst the internal factors would be included such factors as teachers, their values, skills, knowledge and experience, and perceived and felt problems and shortcomings of the existing curriculum.

Alternatively, and focusing on the curriculum in particular, a school could use Scrimshaw's matching pairs of descriptive and narrative questions? These cover the range of objectives and how they are characterized, the values and beliefs underlying that selection of objectives, whether all objectives are for all pupils or only some, and if the latter, how the selection for the individual is made, what 'knowledge-imprints' the components of the curriculum represent and how groupings are related to it and, finally, the methods which are used to evaluate the school's success and how these methods are related to the school's objectives.

One school set about the task pragmatically, looking at the work of the school under four headings: curriculum, including content and resources; pastoral; school culture; teacher attitudes. A small working party was established which looked at these areas in detail with the assistance of other staff more specifically concerned with them. An analysis was made in each area, recommendations were worked out and a report drawn up. The recommendation list from the Schools Council Report *Multicultural Education: The Way Forward* was then quoted and the school report presented to a staff assembly.

It would also be possible for a largely intuitive or impressionistic approach to be adopted and certainly the importance of 'rampant reflection' in the appraisal of education should not be underestimated —or overestimated. But most schools will probably prefer a more systematic analysis, such as or similar to the ones quoted above, which is consistent with their skills and resources, to a rather more subjective approach. Whatever balance they decide on they, that is the school staff, will need to attempt an initial formulation of the kinds of questions they wish to pose and the areas they wish to address. This will certainly include some of the following and no doubt others besides:

1. What are the national and local goals inherent within multicultural education that we should be addressing?
2. What information/evidence do we have of the performance of particular kinds of pupils and how can we take account of it in our planning?
3. What should our policy on multicultural education as a whole, and particular aspects of it such as mother-tongue teaching and English as a second language, be?
4. What is the 'cultural identikit' of our pupils and the community from which they come? What languages and religions are

represented? What cultural values and customs are manifest? What occupations and styles of life?

5. In what ways can the cultural diversity of our pupils and community be meaningfully represented in our school, its organization, curriculum, teaching/learning strategies and examinations? Are our policies for withdrawal groups and referral fair and balanced? Or do they implicitly discriminate against certain cultural groups?

6. What should be the major components of our curriculum and how should these reflect the community of which we are a part? How can they be involved in it?

7. What scope should there be for meaningful representation of pupils, parents and the wider community in the life and decision-making of the school? How can dialogue and discourse be encouraged?

8. Which means should we adopt to evaluate the work of the school and how can we develop culture-fair means of assessing and examining our pupils?

9. How can resources and resource work be maximized and equalized for all pupils?

10. Are our books and teaching materials multicultural value for money? Do they contain inaccurate, racist or discriminatory stereotypes? Are they ethno- or eurocentric or do they seek to offer a wider world view?

11. What policy of staff development do we need in order to support our aspiration to introduce multicultural education and to design and implement a multicultural curriculum and appropriate examinations?

To tackle such questions, one school might establish an initial joint working party to outline and draw up 'the shopping list', and perhaps sketch out an outline policy. Another larger one might envisage a series of working parties to agree particular aspects of the policy and its implementation: mother tongue, the whole curriculum, home-school relations, teaching methods, internal organization and grouping, materials and resources, English as a second language, religious and moral education, mother tongue issues, examinations.[10]

Certainly, what evidence we have would seem to suggest that where such groups are established, they increase corporate awareness and thus provide an essential platform for multicultural education.[11] The idea of sharing explicit within a working party, its collaborative and teamwork approach, probably approximates more closely to the needs of most teachers than does that which is available in more formal course provision. Moreoever, the needs of individual schools are so different that such appraisal as we are suggesting is probably best carried out at school level, although, of course, not without outside assistance and participation. That does not, however, rule out joint enterprise with other institutions and individuals perhaps sometimes in the role of honest broker; nor should it exclude the opportunity for an individual member of staff to do an intensive study of relevance and value to the school, perhaps as part of an advanced study opportunity.

Some suggestions for the individual teacher

The Keele Report on in-service provision for individual teachers speaks of

> ...the experiences of many of the teachers we have interviewed, faced with the day to day and minute by minute problems of working in classrooms with children whose cultural, community, intellectual and linguistic situations are diverse and which they only incompletely understand.

and further:

> ...many teachers have keenly felt professional needs to identify and develop new styles of teaching that are more appropriate for a multicultural society; these include considerable numbers of teachers who are not themselves teaching many pupils from ethnic minority groups.[12]

However good the policy statements and guidelines, it is, in the last resort, on the individual teacher that the full responsibility for the implementation of multicultural education falls. Something of what this involves may be gauged from a recent report. The Interim Rampton Report, for instance, says that teachers should

> be prepared to examine and reappraise their attitudes and behaviour, to challenge all manifestations of racism and to play a learning role in seeking to change the attitudes of society as a whole....[13]

This is a tall order for anyone but particularly for a busy teacher involved in a rapidly changing world, who may be worrying about whether there will be a job at all in the near future and is subject to often conflicting demands and expectations from sometimes strident groups in society. With so many demands and such diverse needs what should be the teacher's priorities in the shorter and longer terms?

To some extent, the answer to this question is what it has always been. The teacher needs to know his/her pupils, know his/her material and resources for teaching and to know his/her job, that is, how to teach.

Under the heading of knowing his/her pupils', he or she will need to take account of socio-cultural background factors such as the home and community as well as such factors as the values and learning styles of the pupils. Under 'material and resources for teaching' comes both curriculum content and examinations as well as the texts and aids which he or she uses.

'Knowing his/her job' means that teachers will have to understand how to motivate and teach in a pluralist classroom where often attitudes to rewards, achievement and life in general are very different from their own. In each of these cases they will need continually to update their knowledge and understanding, acquire new values, develop new skills and be able to demonstrate to themselves, their pupils and their wider professional and lay community that they have climbed this ladder of experience. In other words the reflexivity of their ascent is not only with regard to themselves but also to their pupils and peers. (See Figure 9[14]).

Figure 9
A PLANNING MATRIX FOR INDIVIDUAL TEACHER DEVELOPMENT IN MULTICULTURAL EDUCATION

	Knowledge and Understanding of New Content	Acquisition of New and Changed Attitudes	Development of New Skills and Techniques	Demonstration of New Personal and Social Behaviours
Self				
Pupil/ Community				
Curriculum/ Resources				
Job/ Teaching- Learning Strategies				

As an initial step the teacher might like to pose the following questions:

1. How far does what I teach reflect the diversity of the British multiculture of the 1980s?
2. Is the content free from bias, stereotyping and racism? Is it as fair as I can make it to all cultural groups? Does it eschew

ethnocentrism and eurocentrism and aspire to achieve a world view?

3. Does my teaching deliberately invite the participation of all cultural groups? Do I take the opportunity to show individuals from different cultural groups in different occupational and social roles?

4. Do my teaching strategies enhance the individual pupil's self-worth and respect of others? Both those who are similar to and those who are different from him or her? Do they seek to recognize and comprehend different kinds of motivation and life-views?

5. How do I need to change the content of my teaching to improve the pupils' understanding of their own culture and the heritage of other pupils?

6. Do I draw widely enough on the resource potential of all pupils, staff, parents and the wider community?

7. Do I have equally high academic expectations of pupils from all cultural groups?

8. Do I tend to minimize controversial issues or do I try to tackle them in an open, frank and mature way which invites the contributions of the pupil and plays down my own opinions?

9. Are the materials, texts and displays which I use as free as possible from racism, stereotyping, distortions, patronization, omissions and derogatory language? Do they acknowledge and express the worthy contributions of all cultural groups to national and local life?

10. Are the examinations and assessment methods which I use as culture-fair as possible?

11. Finally, the teacher may wish to ask about ways in which he can help himself. What are my more immediate needs in terms of staff development and where can I obtain assistance?

In terms of this last question, teachers may like to reflect on the grid represented by Figure 9. They may wish to consider whether their most immediate need is for information concerning their own pupils, the composition of the school's community, or content for their curricula – for example, concepts, statistics, descriptive information tasks for analysis, materials from the Commission for Racial Equality and details of sources of information. They may feel they need a more formal course and wish to investigate where this is available and on what terms. If very little has been done they may wish to suggest to the Head and staff the need for a working party to begin to draw up a plan – or even just to begin to 'talk the thing through'.

It is no exaggeration to say that much of the weight of introducing multicultural education falls on the teachers. It will test their skill, expertise and professional commitment to the utmost. Many have already shown that they are fully able to cope with the new perceptions of them and their functions implicit in a multicultural curriculum. But they are only human and sometimes inflated expectations of what they may be able to achieve have been expressed and efforts made to press sectional views as universally acceptable and accepted. Teachers, individually and as a body, can be a very potent influence on the development of a harmonious multicultural society, through a flexible and vital multicultural education. But if much of the rest of society is pulling in the opposite direction, their task is made more difficult, if not impossible.

In the decades since the passage of the 1944 Education Act, teachers have shown themselves well able to change in innumerable different directions: new examinations, new kinds of schools, new curricula, new methods of teaching, new salary structures, new ranges of pupils, both in terms of ability and age, and now, with regard to cultural background, new legislation affecting relations and communications with parents and the community. There is no evidence that they will be unequal to the challenge of the multicultural curriculum, provided other educational and social sectors also play their part in the shared enterprise which is multicultural education.

Summary

This chapter has:

1. identified some of the more immediate tasks in 'getting started' with multicultural education;
2. suggested that it is possible to consider these tasks at system, school and individual levels;
3. proposed items for inclusion in local authority policy statements;
4. referred to three ways of beginning needs-assessment at school level;
5. offered a checklist of items which would be amongst those to be considered by the individual teacher.

Notes and references

1 Multicultural education: the context and the case   pages 9-23

1 A more recent book which gives statistics concerning the changing racial composition of the United Kingdom is: The Runnymede Trust and the Radical Statistics Group, *Britain's Black Population*, Heinemann Educational Books, 1980. Although it is not all-inclusive, the euphemism 'New Commonwealth and Pakistan ethic origin' is used to described Britain's non-European racial groups. See, for example, *Social Trends* 1982, No. 12, page 18, Table 1.9. The lack of unanimity on terminology inhibits more open discussion and indicates the immature stage of comprehension and policy-making.

2 Mulvaney, M., 'Racism and Schools', *Multiethnic Education Review* 1982, 1:1 p. 2.

3 Bullivant, B. M., *The Pluralist Dilemma in Education*, Sydney: George Allen and Unwin, 1981.

4 I have used a similar definition in some of my other writing. See Lynch, J. 'Multicultural Education and the Core Curriculum', *Curriculum* 1982, March, pp. 28-34. In arriving at this tentative definition I have drawn on the definition offered by Gould and Kolb and have been strongly influenced by the arguments concerning 'functional' definitions of culture in the work of Bullivant. See Gould, J. and Kolb, W. L., (eds.) *A Dictionary of the Social Sciences*, Tavistock, 1964, p. 315 (adapted) and Bullivant, B. M., 'The STEPS Case against Multicultural Education: Some Cross-National Findings', in Rowley, G. (ed.) *Proceedings of the 1979 Annual Conference of the Australian Association for Research in Education*, AARE, 1979. I am indebted to Dr. Bullivant for information and ideas provided to me during my stay in Australia and particularly stimulating discussions at Monash University.

5 Hirst, P. H. and Peters, R. S., *The Logic of Education*, Routledge and Kegan Paul, 1970.

6 Jeffcoate, R., 'Curriculum Planning in Multicultural Education', *Educational Research*, 1976, 18:3, pp. 192-200, also reproduced in James, A. and Jeffcoate, R., *The School in the Multicultural Society*, Harper and Row in association with the Open University Press, 1981, pp. 3-18.

7 A recent reaffirmation (and reprint) of Peters's views in easily accessible form is Peters, R. S., *Moral Development and Moral Education*, Allen and Unwin, 1981.

8 Zec, P., 'Multicultural Education: What Kind of Relativism is Possible?', *Journal of Philosophy of Education* (1980), 14:1, pp. 77-86, also reproduced in James and Jeffcoate (1981), op. cit. pp. 29-44.

9 Leach, E., *Social Anthropology*, Fontana, 1982, p. 87.

10 A recent contribution which may herald a welcome renewal of discussion of aims in education and which sees education as aiming at the good of the pupil, the good of others and the good of the economy is White, J. P., *The Aims of Education Restated*, Routledge and Kegan Paul, 1981.

11 Benjamin, H., 'The Sabre-Tooth Curriculum', in Hooper, R., *The Curriculum:*

Context, Design, Development, Oliver and Boyd, 1971, pp. 7-15.

12 The categorization has been deployed in more sophisticated style elsewhere. See Lynch, J., *Education for Community*, Macmillan, 1979, pp. 26 ff and more recently Lawton, D., *Curriculum Planning and Technological Change*, (The Stanley Lecture, 1979), Royal Society of Arts, 1979.

13 By 'primordiality' is meant the culturally assumed givenness of social existence which comes from being born and initiated into a particular kinship, religious or linguistic group.

14 Department of Education and Science, *The School Curriculum*, HMSO, 1981, p. 6.

15 *Ibid.*, p. 3. See also for a brief critique of the aims, White, J., 'Enigmatic Guidelines', in White, J., *et al.*, *No, Minister, A Critique of the D.E.S Paper 'The School Curriculum'*, (Bedford Way Papers 4), University of London Institute of Education, 1981, pp. 9-17.

16 For an elaboration of this argument, see Peters, R. S., *Ethics and Education*, Allen and Unwin, 1966.

17 London Borough of Brent, Primary and Secondary Education Subcommittee 'Report No. 23/81 of the Director of Education'.

18 It will be clear as my argument unfolds that it is derived from the work of Kant, particularly on the 'Categorical Imperative'. See Paton, H. J., *The Moral Law*, Hutchinson, 1972, especially pp. 66-67 and pp. 90-91.

19 Wilson, J., Williams, N., and Sugarman, B., *Introduction to Moral Education*, Penguin, 1967, pp. 76 ff.

20 My thinking on this aspect of my argument has been strongly influenced by the writing of Habermas. With respect to discourse as a means of testing what he calls validity claims, that is, the achievement of a rationally motivated decision concerning the correctness of an argument, he has proposed a number of conditions. See Habermas, J., *Legitimation Crisis*, Heinemann, 1976, translated by Thomas McCarthy, pp. 107-108 *et passim*.

21 Jeffcoate, R., 1976, op. cit.

22 See for example, Elliott, G., 'Self Evaluation and the Teacher', Schools Council and the University of Hull, 1980; Becher, T. *et al.*, *Policies for Educational Accountability*, Heinemann, 1982; Lacey, C., and Lawton, D., *Issues in Evaluation and Accountability*, Methuen, 1981; and recent publications, which include Department of Education and Science, and Welsh Office, *The School Curriculum*, HMSO, 1981 and Circular 6/81. That educational institutions may play a critical role in social change is the major theme of a recent book. See Salter, B., and Tapper, T., *Education, Politics and the State, The Theory and Practice of Educational Change*, Grant MacIntyre, 1982.

23 Schools Council, *The Practical Curriculum. A report from the Schools Council*, (Schools Council Working Paper 70), Methuen Educational, 1981.

24 See for example, Biott, C., 'Pupils Taking Responsibility for the Quality of Discussion', Papers generated by Schools Council Programme Two in Sunderland Local Authority, 1982, mimeo.

2 The teacher and multicultural education   pages 24-54

1 Gordon, N. M., *Assimilation in American Life*, New York: Oxford University Press, 1964.

2 For example, Taft, R., *From Stranger to Citizen*, Nedlands: University of Western Australia Press, 1976; and Richardson, A., 'The Assimilation of Assisted Passage British Immigrants in Australia 1959-66', cyclostyled 1966, quoted in Phillips, D., 'Assimilation Theories as Applied to Immigrants in the Ovens Valley', Canberra: ANU Work in Progress Seminars, Department of Sociology, 1966, cyclostyled. Price's study of migrant groups in the process of chain migration, whilst not of assimilation as such, enables depth to be given to studies of settlement and

integration. See Price, C. A., *Southern Europeans in Australia*, Melbourne: Oxford University Press, 1963.

3 The word is derived from Barnes, D., *From Communication to Curriculum* Harmondsworth: Penguin, 1976 and quoted in Jeffcoate, R., *Positive Image: Towards a multicultural curriculum*, Writers and Readers Publishing Co-operative in association with Chameleon, 1979.

4 Jeffcoate (1979), op. cit., Chapter Three.

5 Jeffcoate (1979), op. cit., p. 46.

6 Bruner, J., 'Man: A Course of Study: Response I', in Stenhouse, L. (ed.), *Curriculum Research and Development in Action*, Heinemann, 1980, p. 225.

7 Inner London Education Authority, *Education in a Multiethnic Society: An Aide Memoire for the Inspectorate*, ILEA, 1981.

8 Taylor, M. J., *Caught Between: A review of research into the education of pupils of West Indian origin*, Windsor, Berks: The NFER-Nelson Publishing Co. Ltd., 1981.

9 Sowell, T., *Ethnic America*, New York: Basic Books, 1981.

10 See for instance Hall, S. J., *Africa in U.S. Educational Materials*, New York: Afro-American Institute, 1976, McDiarmid, G., and Pratt, D., *Teaching Prejudice* Toronto: Ontario Institute for Studies in Education, 1971, and Houston, J., *Let's End the Slander: Combating racial prejudice in teaching materials*, Office of the Commissioner for Community Relations, Canberra: 1979.

11 A useful starter is Schools Council, *Education for a Multiracial Society 5-13* Schools Council, 1981, especially Chapter Eleven. See also Hicks, D., *Images of the World: An Introduction to Bias in Teaching Materials*, University of London Institute of Education, 1980, (Occasional Paper No. 2); Ph.D. thesis 'Textbook Imperialism: A Study of Ethnocentric Bias in Textbooks with Particular Reference to Geography' University of Lancaster, 1980, and a chapter from it published as Hicks, D., 'Bias in Geography Textbooks: Images of the Third World and Multi-Ethnic Britain', Centre for Multicultural Education of the University of London Institute of Education, 1980, Working Paper No. 1. Lists of criteria and guidelines have been produced by the National Union of Teachers, *In Black and White* NUT, 1979, *Children's Book Bulletin* (1979), June, No. 1, pp. 5-8 and Jones, C., and Klein, G., 'Practical Guidelines to Assessing Children's Books for a Multi-Ethnic Society', CUES, n.d.

12 United States Department of Health, Education and Welfare, Office of Education Ethnic Heritage Studies Program, 'Criteria', Mimeo, March, 1981.

13 Green, P., 'Tolerance Teaching and the Self-Concept in the Multiethnic Classroom', *Multiethnic Education Review* (1982), 1:1, pp. 8-11.

14 See Stenhouse, L., et al., *The Problems and Effects of Teaching about Race Relations*, Routledge, 1982 forthcoming and especially chapters VII, VIII and XXII. (I am grateful to Professor Stenhouse for access to the manuscript of his book prior to publication). Two of the early articles on this work are Verma, G. K., and MacDonald, B., 'Teaching Race in Schools: Some Effects on the Attitudinal and Sociometric Patterns of Adolescents', *Race* (1971), 13:2, pp. 187-202, and Verma, G. K., and Bagley, C., 'Changing Racial Attitudes and Adolescents: An Experimental English Study', *International Journal of Psychology* (1976), 8:1, pp. 55-8.

15 Banks, J. A., 'Reducing Prejudice in Students: Theory, Research and Strategies', paper presented at Simon Fraser University, Burnaby, British Columbia, February 3, 1982, pp. 20-21.

16 'Editorial', *Multiracial Education* (1981), 9:2, p. 1. The whole issue was devoted to race and the media. See also Downing, J., *The Media Machine*, Pluto, 1980, which argues that media portrayal of race, sex and class is a means of stabilizing capitalist society around what are basically sexist and racist values. An interesting study in the United States is Banks, C.A.M., 'A Content Analysis of the Treatment of Black Americans on Television', *Social Education* (1977), April, pp. 336-339.

17 A similar response was elicited to the survey which was a preliminary to the Schools Council Project 'Education for a Multiracial Society', See Townsend, H. E. R., and Brittan, E. M., *Multiracial Education: Need and Innovation*, Evans/Methuen, 1973, p. 83. (Schools Council Working Paper 50).

18 Banks, J. A., *Multiethnic Education: Theory and Practice*, Boston, Mass: Allyn and Bacon, Inc., 1981.

19 Miller, H. J., 'A study of the effectiveness of a variety of teaching techniques for reducing colour prejudice in a male student sample aged 15-21'. University of London M.A. Thesis, 1967, and Miller, H. J., 'The effectiveness of teaching techniques for reducing colour prejudice', *Liberal Education* (1969), 16, p. 25, and Banks (1982), op. cit.

20 Hall, S., 'Teaching Race', *Multiracial Education* (1981), 9:1. pp. 3-13.

21 I am indebted to the work of Banks for the formulation contained in this sentence. See Banks, J. A., *Teaching Strategies for Ethnic Studies* (2nd ed.), Boston: Allyn and Bacon, 1981.

22 The Schools Council, *The Humanities Project: An Introduction*, Heinemann Educational Books, 1970.

23 Stenhouse, L., *An Introduction to Curriculum Research and Development*, Heinemann, 1975, p. 24 and p. 39.

24 Ibid., p. 213.

25 Stenhouse, L., 'Research as a Basis for Teaching', *Inaugural Lecture* given at the University of East Anglia, Norwich, 29 February 1979. The reader may wish to dwell at greater length on this and Chapter Ten of Stenhouse (1975) cited above.

26 Schools Council, *Raising the School Leaving Age: A Co-operative Programme of Research and Development*, HMSO, 1965, para. 97, (Working Papers 2), quoted in Aston, A., 'The Humanities Curriculum Project', in Stenhouse, L., *Curriculum Research and Development in Action*, Heinemann, 1980, p. 140.

27 Rudduck, J., *Learning to Teach Through Discussion*, Norwich: Centre for Applied Research in Education, 1979.

28 Ibid., pp. 11-13. It is difficult without plagiarizing to give an impression of the full richness and practical usefulness of this slender account of the 'how' of curriculum development and I would hope that the reader would look for him/herself at the publication and use it.

29 Sikes, P. (ed.), *Teaching about Race Relations*, Norwich: National Association for Race Relations Teaching and Action Research, CARE, University of East Anglia, 1979.

30 Ibid., pp. 1-2.

31 Ibid., pp. 3-14.

32 King, E. W., *Teaching Ethnic Awareness*, Santa Monica, California: Goodyear Publishing Company Inc., 1980.

33 Grant, G., *The Praise of Diversity: Multicultural Classroom Applications*, Omaha, Nebraska: University of Nebraska Centre for Urban Education, n.d.

34 Garcia, R. L., *Teaching in a Pluralistic Society: Concepts, models, strategies*, New York: Harper and Row, 1982.

35 Hansen-Krening, N., *Competency and Creativity in Language Arts: A multiethnic focus*, Reading, Mass.: Addison-Wesley Publishing Co., 1979.

36 Gibson, M. A., 'Approaches to Multicultural Education in the United States: Some Concepts and Assumptions', *Anthropology and Education Quarterly* (1976), 7:4, pp. 7-18.

37 Williams, J., 'Perspectives on the Multicultural Curriculum', *The Social Science Teacher* (1979), 8:4, pp. 126-133.

38 Lynch, J., 'Multicultural Teacher Education in Australia: The State of the Art'. (A report submitted to the Education Research and Development Committee), Canberra: ERDC, 1980, cyclostyled p. 120.

39 House of Commons, Home Affairs Committee, *Fifth Report: Racial Disadvantage*,

HMSO, 1981, vol. I, p. LXVI, para. 155.

40 See, for example, Wilding, J., *Ethnic Minority Languages in the Classroom*, Leicester: Leicester City Council, Council for Community Relations, 1981.

41 Little, A., and Willey, R., *Multiethnic Education: The Way Forward*, Schools Council, 1981, p. 20.

42 Schools Council, *Education for a Multiracial Society: Curriculum and context 5-13*, Schools Council, 1981.

43 Wright, L., and Hanson, L., 'Bradford Multicultural Education Project: Suggestions for a Project on Food', Bradford: n.d. (1979?) and 'Bradford Multicultural Education Project: Suggested Notes for Teachers', Bradford: n.d. (1979?).

44 Birley High School, 'Multicultural Education in the 1980s', Manchester: City of Manchester Education Committee, 1980.

45 Dummett, A., 'Educating for Unifying Culture', *The Times* (1974), 9 July, quoted in Schools Council (1981), op. cit., p. 9.

46 Schools Council (1981), op. cit., p. 11.

47 Jeffcoate, R., *Positive Image: Towards a multiracial curriculum*, Richmond, Surrey: Chameleon, 1979, p. 26, *et passim*.

48 Jeffcoate, R., 'Curriculum Planning in Multiracial Education', James, A. and Jeffcoate, R. (eds.), *The School in the Multicultural Society*, Harper and Row, 1981, pp. 3-18.

49 Bullivant, B. M., *Race, Ethnicity and Curriculum*, Melbourne: Macmillan, 1981.

50 Ibid., pp. 86-101.

51 Smolicz, J. J., *Culture and Education in a Plural Society*, Canberra: Curriculum Development Centre, 1979, pp. 235-271.

52 Smolicz, J. J., op. cit., pp. 267-269.

53 Banks, J. A., *Multiethnic Education: Theory and practice*, Boston: Allyn and Bacon, 1981, p. 97.

54 Curriculum Development Centre, Canberra, *Core Curriculum for Australian Schools: What it is and why it is needed*, Canberra: CDC, 1980, p. 15.

55 Birley High School, 'Multicultural Education in the 1980s', Manchester: City of Manchester Education Committee, 1980, loc. cit., p. 2. There is an increasing number of such school generated multicultural curricula and evidence, quoted above, that large numbers of schools and teachers are involved in such curricularizing. Some examples are given in Twitchin, J., and Demuth, C., *Multicultural Education: Views from the classroom*, BBC, 1981 and especially Chapter Seven.

3 A framework for multicultural education   pages 55-83

1 See in particular Peters, R. S., *Ethics and Education*, Allen and Unwin, 1966.

2 See in particular Lawton, D., *An Introduction to Teaching and Learning*, Hodder and Stoughton, 1981, and Stenhouse, L., *An Introduction to Curriculum Research and Development*, Heinemann, 1975.

3 London Borough of Brent Teachers Association, *Multicultural Education in Brent Schools*, Brent, June 1980, p. 11.

4 Schools Council, *Education of Children from Ethnic Minority Groups*, Schools Council, 1982, p. 12, (Schools Council Pamphlet 19).

5 Bruner, J., *Toward a Theory of Instruction*, Cambridge, Mass.: Harvard University Press, 1966.

6 Secretary of State for Education and Science, Secretary of State for Wales. *Education in Schools: A Consultative Document*, HMSO, 1977, (Cmnd 6869) pp. 6-7. A very useful rehearsal of the multicultural aims of a range of official documents is contained in a recent Schools Council publication. See Willey, R., *Teaching in Multicultural Britain*, Schools Council, 1982.

7 It was even commended, 'without further refinements, as a checklist against which

local authorities and schools can test their curricular policies and their application to individual schools'. See Department of Education and Science and Welsh Office, *The School Curriculum*, HMSO, 1981, pp. 3-4. See also the precursor document from the same source, *A Framework for the School Curriculum*, DES and Welsh Office, 1980.

8 White, J., 'Enigmatic Guidelines' in White, J., et al., *No Minister: A Critique of the DES Paper 'The School Curriculum'*, University of London Institute of Education, 1981 pp. 9-17. (Bedford Way Papers, 4).

9 Curriculum Development Centre, *Core Curriculum for Australian Schools*, Canberra: CDC, 1980, p. 9.

10 Ibid., pp. 10-11.

11 Townsend, H. E. R. and Brittan, E. M., *Multiracial Education: Need and Innovation*, Evans/Methuen, 1973, (Schools Council Working Paper 50).

12 See 'Handbook Disowned by Authors', *The Times Educational Supplement* (1981), 26 June, p. 3.

13 Eisner, E., 'Instructional and Expressive Educational Objectives' *Instructional Objectives*, AERA Monograph 3, 1969, pp. 16-17.

14 Schools Council, *Multicultural Education* (1982), p. 10.

15 Schools Council, *Education for a Multiracial Society: Curriculum and Context 5-13*, Schools Council, 1981, p. 18.

16 The Schools Council Communication and Social Skills Project Report has a useful listing of the kinds of 'implementation' aims which could usefully be subsumed under these headings. See Lorac, C., and Weiss, M., *Communication and Social Skills*, Exeter: Wheaton, 1981, particularly Appendix 1, pp. 188-201.

17 The concept of ethclass is taken from the work of an Australian academic which looked at the relations between family learning environments, academic performance and attitudes to school of 414 girls and 436 boys from different ethclasses, defined as representing the intersection of horizontal and vertical divisions of society into social status groups and ethnic groups. See Marjoribanks, K., *Ethnic Families and Children's Achievements*, Sydney: George Allen and Unwin, 1979, p. 11.

18 Schools Council, *Multicultural Education*, March 1982, p. 4.

19 Stenhouse, L., *An Introduction to Curriculum Research and Development*, Heinemann, 1975, p. 8.

20 Musgrave, P.W., *The Sociology of Education*, 3rd edition, Methuen, 1979, p. 200.

21 Propounded in Hirst, P. H., 'Liberal Education and the Nature of Knowledge', in Archambault, R. D. (ed.), *Philosophical Analysis and Education*, Routledge and Kegan Paul, 1965.

22 Habermas, J., *Knowledge and Human Interests*, translated by Jeremy J. Shapiro, 2nd edition, Heinemann, 1978, p. 313.

23 The account of this formulation given by Lawton is well worth reading. See Lawton, D., *The Politics of the School Curriculum*, Routledge and Kegan Paul, 1980, pp. 50ff. For a succinct and helpful discussion of different models of curriculum planning, see Lawton, D., *An Introduction to Teaching and Learning*, Hodder and Stoughton, 1981, especially Chapter Seven.

24 Her Majesty's Inspectorate, *Curriculum 11-16*, 1977, p. 6.

25 Curriculum Development Centre, *Core Curriculum for Australian Schools*, Canberra; CDC, 1980, p. 11.

26 Ibid., pp. 18-19.

27 Ibid., p. 16.

28 Dale, E., *Audio-Visual Methods in Teaching*, New York: Holt, Rinehart and Winston, 1965, Chapter Four.

29 See, for example, much of the material produced by the Further Education Research and Development Unit at the Department of Education and Science in the social education and social and life skills areas, such as Further Education Research and

Development Unit, *Developing Social and Life Skills*, FEU/DES, 1980, or the excellent resume *Beyond Coping: Some approaches to social education*, FEU/DES, 1980.

30 Gagné, R. M., *The Conditions of Learning*, Holt, Rinehart and Winston, 3rd edition, 1979. A similar, but slightly different categorization is contained in Schools Council, *Education of Children from Ethnic Minority Groups* (1982), op. cit., p. 11.

31 This is a particularly neglected aspect in school curriculum. See Kahn, N., *The Arts Britain Ignores*, Commission for Racial Equality, 1976 and the more recent HMI Report, concerning art in multiethnic comprehensive schools, Department of Education and Science, 'Aspects of Organisation and Curriculum in Seven Multi-Ethnic Comprehensive Schools', DES, 1979. More recently still, proposals have been made, however, for the inclusion of ethnic arts in 'O' and 'A' level examinations. See Commission for Racial Equality, *Arts Education in a Multicultural Society*, CRE, 1981, p. 3.

32 Bullivant, B. M., *Race, Ethnicity and Curriculum*, Melbourne: Macmillan, 1981, p. 71.

33 Bantock, G. H., *Dilemmas of the Curriculum*, Oxford: Martin Robertson, 1980, pp. 128-129.

34 See for instance, Cole, M., and Bruner, J. S., 'Preliminaries to a Theory of Cultural Differences', in National Society for the Study of Education, *Yearbook*, Chicago: University of Chicago, 1972.

35 See an early exposé of this 'deficit' explanation in Coard, B., *How the West Indian Child is Made Educationally Subnormal in the British School System*, New Beacon Books, 1971. See also an interesting study by Driver of the performance of English, West Indian and Asian school leavers at 16+. Driver, D., *Beyond Underachievement*, Commission for Racial Equality, 1980, Giles's classic study, Giles, R., *The West Indian Experience in British Schools*, Heinemann, 1977.

36 Stone, M., *The Education of the Black Child in Britain*, Fontana, 1981.

37 Carrington, B., 'Schooling an Underclass: The Implications of Ethnic Differences in Attainment', *Durham and Newcastle Research Review* (1981), IX:47, pp. 293-305.

38 I have drawn some of these procedural principles in amended form from Maryland State Department of Education, *New Perspectives in Intergroup Education*, Baltimore, Maryland: Division of Instruction, 1975, p. 20.

39 Amongst those who have advanced the process models as opposed to alternative 'pupil-achievement' focused models are McDonald, B., 'Accountability, Standards and the Process of Schooling', in Becher, T., and Maclure, S., *Accountability in Education*, Slough: NFER, 1978, and Elliott, J., 'Who Should Monitor Performance in Schools?', in Sockett, H., *Accountability in the English Educational System*, Hodder and Stoughton, 1980.

40 We are fortunate in having a number of papers which tackle the crucial issue of the demands which this kind of evaluation makes on teachers and the kind of training provided. See, for example, Simons, H., 'Process Evaluation in Schools', in Lacey, C., and Lawton, D., *Issues in Evaluation and Accountability*, Methuen, 1981, and Biott, C., 'Training Students for Careers in Self-Evaluating Schools: Apprenticeship in classroom action research', *Classroom Action Research Bulletin* (1982), No. 5. I am grateful to Colin Biott for an advance copy of this paper.

41 Inner London Education Authority, *Education in a Multiethnic Society: An aide-memoire for the Inspectorate*, County Hall, 1981.

42 National Study of School Evaluation, *Evaluation Guidelines for Multicultural/Multiracial Education*, Arlington, Va: National Study of School Evaluation, 1973.

43 National Council for the Social Studies, *Curriculum Guidelines for Multiethnic Education*, Arlington, Va: NCSS, 1976, pp. 42-48.

44 National Education Association, *Profiles of Excellence: How to establish racial*

equality in schools, Washington DC: NEA, 1980.
45 Nuttall, D. L., *School Self-Evaluation: Accountability with a human face?*, Schools Council, 1981.

4 The community and the multicultural school pages 84-101

1 Central Advisory Council for Education, *Early Learning*, HMSO, 1954.
2 Central Advisory Council for Education (England), *Half Our Future (The Newsom Report)*, HMSO, 1963, pp. 70 (para. 204) and 71.
3 Schools Council, *Young School Leavers (Enquiry 1)*, HMSO, 1968, p. 242.
4 Central Advisory Council for Education (England), *Children and their Primary Schools* (The Plowden Report), HMSO, 1967, p. 48.
5 Lynch, J., and Pimlott, J., *Parents and Teachers*, Macmillan Education, 1976, pp. 72-73.
6 Department of Education and Science, *A Language for Life (The Bullock Report)*, HMSO, 1975, para. 20.16, p. 293.
7 Ibid., p. 545.
8 Department of Education and Science, Welsh Office, *A New Partnership of Our Schools (The Taylor Report)*, HMSO, 1977.
9 Ibid., p. 126.
10 Ibid., pp. 114-115.
11 Driver, G., 'Cultural Competence, Social Power and School Achievement', *New Community* (1977) Spring/Summer.
12 Hammersley, M., 'The Mobilisation of Pupil Attention', in Hammersley, M., and Woods, P. (eds.), *The Process of Schooling*, Routledge and Kegan Paul, 1976.
13 Verma, G. K., and Bagley, C. (eds.), *Race and Education across Cultures*, Heinemann, 1975.
14 It is important to make absolutely clear that such 'racist' explanations are refuted by all responsible teacher associations. See, for example, National Union of Teachers, *Race, Education, Intelligence: A teacher's guide to the facts and the issues*, NUT, 1978.
15 An interesting study, using the concept of 'caste' as an explanation of minority and dominant group competence as part of a broader paradigm, in Ogbu, J., *Minority Education and Caste: The American System in Cross-Cultural Perspective*, New York: Academic Press, 1978.
16 Department of Education and Science, Report by HM Inspectors on *Aspects of Organisation and Curriculum in Seven Multiethnic Comprehensive Schools*, DES, 1979, p. 9.
17 United Kingdom, Parliament, *Education Act 1980*, HMSO, 1980, §8 in particular.
18 Department of Education and Science, *Statutory Instruments*, 1981, No. 630, HMSO, 1981. See also a useful Schools Council summary, Schools Council, *Home School Communications*, 1981.
19 Department of Education and Science, *West Indian Children in Our Schools* (The Rampton Report), HMSO, 1981, p. 41.
20 Taylor, M. J., *Caught Between: A Review of Research into the Education of Pupils of West Indian Origin*, NFER-Nelson, 1981, p. 149.
21 House of Commons, Home Affairs Committee, *Fifth Report (Racial Disadvantage)*, HMSO, 1981, vol. 1, p. 1xiii.
22 Rex, J., 'Culture Clashes', *Times Educational Supplement* (1981), 7 August, p. 4.
23 Ealing Community Relations Council, *Race Relations and the Secondary School Curriculum*, Commission for Racial Equality, March 1980.
24 Hargreaves, D., 'In Search of Competence', *Times Educational Supplement* (1982), 2 April, p. 19, and *The Challenge for the Comprehensive School: Culture, Curriculum and Community*, Routledge and Kegan Paul, 1982.
25 Inner London Education Authority, *Multi-Ethnic Education* (Joint report of the

Schools Sub-Committee and the Further and Higher Education Sub-Committee), presented to the Education Committee on 8 November 1977, County Hall, 1977.

26 An interesting reflection of the social imperatives introduced in Chapter One and used in a journal editorial, is Preston, M., 'Premix Concrete', *Curriculum* (1982), 3:1, p. 4.

27 See House of Commons, Home Affairs Committee, Session 1980-81, *Racial Disadvantage* (Volume II, Evidence), HMSO, 1981, pp. 41-159, passim.

28 Ibid., p. 159.

29 Ibid., p. 153.

30 House of Commons, Home Affairs Committee, Session 1980-81, *Racial Disadvantage* (Volume III, Evidence), HMSO, 1981, pp. 1024-1026. The experimental community rooms established in the past four years by Sheffield are an analogous if functionally rather different development. See Jane Mackillop, *Ethnic Minorities in Sheffield*, Sheffield Metropolitan Education Committee, n.d., p. 75.

31 Ibid.

32 Craft, M., E351: Educational Studies, A Third Level Course, *Urban Education*, Block Two, p. 135, The Open University Press, 1974.

33 London Borough of Brent, Primary and Secondary Education Sub-Committee, 'Report No. 23/81 of the Director of Education: Multicultural Education in Brent', p. 7.

34 Ibid.

35 Schools Council, *The New Approach to the Social Studies: Continuity and development in children's learning through First, Middle and High School*, Schools Council Publications, 1981.

36 Parekh, B., 'Sympathetic Imagination and the Multicultural Curriculum' in Twitchin, J., and Demuth, C., *Multi-Cultural Education: Views from the classroom*, British Broadcasting Corporation, 1981, pp. 83-90.

37 Schools Council, *Education for a Multiracial Society*, Schools Council, 1981, p. 9.

38 Lynch, J., *Education for Community: A Cross-Cultural Study in Education*, Macmillan, 1979.

39 Habermas, J., *Toward a Rational Society* (Translated by Jeremy Shapiro), Heinemann, 1971, pp. 91-4.

40 Birley High School, *Multicultural Education in the 1980s*, Manchester: City of Manchester Education Committee, May 1980, p. 39.

41 National Association for Teaching English as a Second Language to Adults, *English as a Second Language Teaching for Adults from Ethnic Minorities*, Isleworth, Middlesex: NATELSA, 1981.

42 Leicester Council for Community Relations, *Ethnic Minority Languages in the Classroom: A Survey of Asian Parents in Leicester*, Leicester City Council, 1981.

43 National Association for Multiracial Education, 'Policy Statement: Mother Tongue and Minority Community Languages in Education', Mickleover, Derby: n.d. (1981?).

44 Stone, M., *The Education of the Black Child in Britain*, Fontana, 1981, 170ff.

45 Little, A., and Willey, R., *Multi-ethnic Education: The Way Forward*, Schools Council, 1981, (Schools Pamphlet 18).

46 Schools Council, *The Practical Curriculum*, Schools Council, Methuen Educational, 1981, p. 66.

47 Hills, K., 'The Operation of a Multicultural Secondary School', in D'Oyley, V. (ed.), *The Impact of Multi-Ethnicity on Canadian Education*, Toronto, Ontario: The Urban Alliance on Race Relations (Educational Institutions Project), 1977, pp. 121-127.

48 See Hewison, J., 'Home is where the help is', *Times Educational Supplement* (1981), 16 January. The action research appeared to indicate that such parental involvement was more efficacious than considerable extra teaching in school.

49 This list is based on a selection of items taken from (and amended) New South Wales, Department of Education, 'Multicultural Education Policy Statement', Sydney: 1979, pp. 1-2, Part 2, mimeo.
50 Readers may wish to refer once again to the Schools Council document, see Nuttall, D. L., *School Self-Evaluation: Accountability with a human face?*, Schools Council, 1981. (Report and commentary on a Schools Council Conference held at Stoke Rochford Hall, 23-26 February 1981).

5 Resources for multicultural curriculum development   pages 102-18

1 See for instance Hicks, D. W., *Minorities: A Teachers Resource Book for the Multiethnic Curriculum*, Heinemann, 1981.
2 Klein, G., *Resources for Multicultural Education: An Introduction*, Schools Council, 1982.
3 Reported in Matthews, A., *Advisory Approaches to Multicultural Education*, Runnymede Trust, 1981, p. 51.
4 Eggleston, S. J., et al., *In-Service Teacher Education in a Multiracial Society*, Keele, Staffs: The University, 1981, p. 336.
5 Ibid., p. 363.
6 Teachers will wish to note the response of the Government to the proposals of the Select Committee on Racial Disadvantage in this respect. See Secretary of State for the Home Department, *The Government Reply to the Fifth Report from the Home Affairs Committee Session 1980-81 HC424: Racial Disadvantage*, HMSO, 1982, p. 13.
7 NCBE, 1300 Wilson Boulevard, Suite 132-11, Rosslyn Virginia, 22209, USA. The Clearinghouse has now inaugurated a computerized database about current research studies relevant to bilingual education which includes prepublished materials, and is entitled BROL (Bilingual Research on Line).
8 Ethnic Heritage Studies Clearinghouse and Social Science Education Consortium Inc., 855 Broadway, Boulder, Colorado, 80302, USA.
9 Australian Institute of Multicultural Affairs, *Review of Multicultural and Migrant Education*, Melbourne: 1980. (Address, 570 Bourke Street, Melbourne 3000, Australia).
10 Schools Commission, Resources for Schools: *Multicultural Education*, Melbourne: 1978, revised edition, and Education Department of Tasmania, *Resources for Multicultural Education*, Hobart, Tasmania: 1979.
11 Taylor, F., *Race, School and Community: A Survey of Research and Literature on Education in Multiracial Britain*, NFER, 1974. Commission for Racial Equality, *World Religions: A Handbook for Teachers*, CRE, 1976.
12 The Runnymede Trust, *Ethnic Minorities in Britain: A select bibliography*, The Runnymede Trust, 1979 and Hicks, D. W., *Minorities: A Teachers Resource Book for the Multiethnic Curriculum* (1981), op. cit.
13 Lynch, J. (ed.), *Teaching in the Multicultural School*, Ward Lock, 1981.
14 Schools Council, *Education for a Multiracial Society*, 1981.
15 Elkin, J., *Multiracial Books for the Classroom*, Library Association, 1980.
16 Taylor, M., *Caught Between: A Review of Research into the Education of Pupils of West Indian Origin*, NFER-Nelson, 1981.
17 Commission for Racial Equality, Elliot House, 10/12 Allington Street, London SW1E 5EH.
18 Addresses:
National Association for Multiracial Education (NAME), 86 Station Road, Mickleover, Derby, DE3 5ST.
National Committee on Racism in Children's Books, 240 Lancaster Road, London W11.
Children's Rights Workshop, 4 Alderbert Terrace, London SW8.

19 Centre for Urban Educational Studies (CUES), Robert Montefiore Building, Underwood Road, London E1 5AD.

20 Schools Council, *Multicultural Education*, March, 1982.

21 Schols Council, *Multiracial Education: need and innovation*, Schools Council, 1973 and *Education for a Multiracial Society*, Schools Council, 1981, quoted above.

22 See Lorac, C., and Weiss, M., *Communication and Social Skills*, Wheaton, 1981.

23 Centre for Applied Research in Education (CARE), University of East Anglia, Norwich NR4 7TJ.

24 See, for example, Further Education Curriculum Review and Development Unit, *Developing Social and Life Skills*, January 1980, and *A Basis for Choice*, June, 1979.

25 See, for example, Teachers' Notes, *People Around Us: Families*, A. & C. Black and ILEA Learning Materials Services.

26 James, A., and Jeffcoate, R. (eds.), *The School in the Multiracial Society*, Harper and Row, 1981.

27 Morrish, I., *The Background of Immigrant Pupils*, Allen and Unwin, 1971.

28 the Runnymede Trust and the Radical Statistics Race Group, *Britain's Black Population*, Heinemann, 1981.

29 See, for example, Office of Population Censuses and Surveys, *Immigration Statistics: Sources and Definitions*, OPCS, 1979, (Occasional Paper 15).

30 Bullivant, B., *The Pluralist Dilemma in Education*, Sydney: George Allen and Unwin, 1981 and *Race, Ethnicity and Curriculum*, Melbourne: Macmillan, 1981. An alternative model of curriculum construction from the Antipodes is Claydon, L., et al., *Curriculum and Culture: Schooling in a pluralistic society*, Sydney: George Allen and Unwin, 1977.

31 Banks, J. A., *Multiethnic Education: Theory and Practice*, Boston: Allyn and Bacon, 1981 and *Teaching Strategies for Ethnic Studies*, Boston: Allyn and Bacon, 1979 (2nd edition).

32 Mallea, J. R., and Shea, E. C., *Multiculturalism and Education*, Toronto, Ontario: Ontario Institute for Studies in Education and The Ontario Ministry of Culture and Recreation, 1979.

33 Maxwell, J., et al., *Resource List for a Multicultural Society*, Toronto, Ontario: Ministry of Education and Ministry of Culture and Recreation, 1976. See also more recent Occasional Papers in the series from the Centre for the Study of Curriculum and Instruction at the University of British Columbia.

34 Stenhouse, L., *An Introduction to Curriculum Research and Development*, Heinemann, 1975, and Stenhouse, L. (ed.), *Curriculum Research and Development in Action*, Heinemann, 1980.

35 See, for instance, Reynolds, J., and Skilbeck, M., *Culture and the Classroom*, Open Books, 1976 and the newer Open University Curriculum Course E203.

36 Lawton, D., *The Politics of the School Curriculum*, Routledge, 1980 and *An Introduction to Teaching and Learning*, Hodder and Stoughton, 1981.

37 Tawney, D. (ed.), *Curriculum Evaluation Today*, Macmillan Education, 1976.

38 Hamilton, D., *Curriculum Evaluation*, Open Books, 1976.

39 Schools Council, *An Introduction to Evaluation: Some Notes for Schools Council Evaluators*, Schools Council, 1979.

40 Elliott, J., and MacDonald, B. (eds.), *People in Classrooms*, Centre for Applied Research in Education at the University of East Anglia, 1975 (Occasional Paper No. 2).

41 Craft, M. (ed.), *Teaching in a Multicultural Society: The Task for Teacher Education*, Brighton: The Falmer Press, 1981.

42 Eggleston, S. J., et al., *In-Service Teacher Education in a Multi-Racial Society*, Keele, Staffs: University of Keele, 1981.

43 Commission for Racial Equality, *Teacher Education for a Multiracial Society*, CRE, 1974 (2nd edition, 1978), *In-Service Education of Teachers in Multiracial Areas*, CRE, 1974 (reprinted March 1980).

44 See, for example, Lee, M. (compiler), *Multicultural Teacher Education: An Annotated Bibliography of Selected Resources*, Washington, DC: American Association of Colleges for Teacher Education, 1980.

45 London Borough of Brent, 'Multicultural Education in Brent Schools', 1980. Harringay and Holloway have produced statements as well. See the list in Klein (1982), op. cit.

46 Inner London Education Authority, *Education in a Multiethnic Society: An Aide Memoire for the Inspectorate*, 1981.

47 Birley High School, Manchester, *Multicultural Education in the 1980s*, Manchester: City of Manchester Education Committee, 1980.

48 Rose, E. J. B., et al., *Colour and Citizenship*, Oxford University Press, 1969, and Milner, D., *Children and Race*, Penguin, 1975.

49 Home Office, *The Brixton Disorders, 10-12 April 1981*, HMSO, 1981 (Cmnd. 8427).

50 Home Office, *Ethnic Minorities in Britain* (Home Office Research Study No. 68), HMSO, 1981.

51 Ibid., p. 5.

52 House of Commons, Home Affairs Committee, *Fifth Report: Racial Disadvantage*, HMSO, 1981, vols. I-IV.

53 Secretary of State for the Home Department, *The Government Reply to the Fifth Report from the Home Affairs Committee Session 1980-81 HC 424: Racial Disadvantage*, HMSO, 1982.

54 National Union of Teachers, *Race, Education, Intelligence*, 1978. See also the pamphlet *Section 11: An NUT Report*, 1978.

55 Flynn, J. R., *Race, IQ and Jensen*, Routledge and Kegan Paul, 1980.

56 Jeffcoate, R., *Positive Image: Towards a Multiracial Curriculum*, Chameleon Books, 1979.

57 Lester, A., and Bindman, G., *Race and Law*, Penguin, 1972.

58 See, for example, the early work in this field by Bhatnagar, J., *Immigrants at School*, Cornmarket Press, 1970.

59 Townsend, H. E. R., *Immigrant Pupils in England: The LEA Response*, NFER, 1971 and Townsend, H. E. R., and Brittan, E. M., *Organization in Multiracial Schools*, NFER, 1972.

60 House of Commons, Select Committee on Race Relations and Immigration, *Education*, HMSO, 1973, and *The West Indian Community*, HMSO, 1977.

61 Little, A., and Willey, R., *Multiethnic Education: The Way Forward*, Schools Council, 1981 (Schools Council Pamphlet 18).

62 NUT, *In Black and White*, 1979.

63 Whitehead, F., *Children and their Books*, Macmillan Education, 1977.

64 Searle, C., *The Forsaken Lover: White Words and Black People*, Penguin, 1973, and *The World in a Classroom*, Writers and Readers Publishing Co-operative, 1977.

65 Derrick, J., *Language Needs of Minority Group Children*, NFER, 1977.

66 Garvie, E., *Breakthrough to Fluency: English as a second language for young children*, Blackwell, 1976.

67 Edwards, V., *The West Indian Language Issue in British Schools: challenges and responses*, Routledge and Kegan Paul, 1979.

68 Barnes, D., and Todd, F., *Communication and Learning in Small Groups*, Routledge and Kegan Paul, 1977.

69 Tough, J., *Talking and Learning*, Ward Lock Educational in Association with Drake Educational Associates, 1977, reprinted 1979.

70 Candlin, C., and Derrick, J., *Language*, CRE, 1977.

71 Smith, E., *Some Aspects of Story-Telling in Second Language Teaching*, CRE, 1979, reprint.

72 See Rees, O. A., and Fitzpatrick, F., papers of the Mother Tongue and English Teaching Project (MOTET), Bradford University/Bradford College, 1980.

142 Notes and references

73 Fitzpatrick, F., 'The Language Question in the Multiracial School', *Multiracial Education* (1981), 10:1, pp. 3-20

74 Khan, V. S., *Bilingualism and Linguistic Minorities in Britain: Developments, Perspectives*, Runnymede Trust, 1978.

75 Baker, K. A., and de Kanter, A. A., 'Effectiveness of Bilingual Education: A Review of the Literature', (Final Draft Report), United States Department of Education, September 1981, available from NCBE, Rosslyn, Va., USA.

76 c/o Lambeth Teachers' Centre, Santley Street, London SW4.

77 National Membership Secretary, Kathleen Langmore, 59 Station Road, Codsall, Wolverhampton WV8 1BY.

78 AFFOR, 173 Lazells Road, Birmingham B19 1RN.

79 Benjamin Franklin House, 36 Craven Street, London WC2.

80 Commonwealth Institute, Kensington High Street, London W8 6NQ. (In Scotland, 8 Rutland Square, Edinburgh).

81 For an initial list, see National Union of Teachers, *Treasure Chest for Teachers*, NUT, 1981.

82 Publishing Centre, Highbury Station Road, London N1 1SB; Television Centre, Thackeray Road, London SW8 3TB.

83 ACER Project, 275 Kennington Lane, London SE11 5QZ.

84 International Centre for Multicultural Education (ICME), Centre for Advanced Studies in Education, 7 Church Road, Edgbaston, Birmingham.

85 CILT, 20 Carlton Terrace, London SW1.

86 IRR, 247 Pentonville Road, N1.

87 Centre for World Development Education, 128 Buckingham Palace Road, London SW1.

88 Centre for Peace Studies, St Martin's College, Lancaster LA1 3JD.

89 National Extension College, 18 Brooklands Avenue, Cambridge.

90 Runnymede Trust, 37A Grays Inn Road, London WC1.

6 The multicultural curriculum: some guidelines for action   pages 119-29

1 I have drawn on a number of such policy statements in Britain and abroad for ideas for inclusion. In addition to those mentioned before, these include State of Iowa, Department of Public Instruction, *Guide to Implementing Multicultural, Non-Sexist Curriculum Programmes in Iowa Schools*, Des Moines, Iowa: Department of Public Instruction, 1976; Seattle School Board, *District Goals and Objectives 1980-81*, Seattle: 1980; California State Department of Education, *Planning for Multicultural Education as a Part of School Improvement*, Sacramento, California: 1979, and cyclostyled copies of bilingual and multicultural education policies.

2 Lord Scarman's comments are particularly appropriate in this respect. See Home Office, *The Brixton Disorders, 10-12 April 1981* (The Scarman Report), HMSO, 1981, p. 9, p. 106. *et passim* (Cmnd. 8427).

3 Matthews, A., *Advisory Approaches to Multicultural Education*, The Runnymede Trust, 1981, p. 51.

4 Ibid., pp. 50-51.

5 Eggleston, S. J., *In-Service Teacher Education in a Multiracial Society*, Keele, Staffs: University of Keele, 1981, p. 334.

6 Ibid.

7 Stenhouse, L., 'Towards a Vernacular Humanism', Dartington Hall Conference Papers, 1978.

8 Reynolds, J., and Skilbeck, M., *Culture and the Classroom*, Open Books, 1976, pp. 109-115.

9 Scrimshaw, P., et al., *Towards the Whole Curriculum*, The Open University Press, 1976, pp. 10-13 (Open University Course E203: Curriculum Design and Development, Unit 9).

10 A recent helpful document for teachers is: Schools Council, *Examining in a Multicultural Society* (The Report of the Conference held at the Schools Council, 25 September 1981), Schools Council, December 1981.
11 Department of Education and Science, *Aspects of Organisation and Curriculum in Seven Multiethnic Comprehensive Schools*, DES. 1979.
12 Eggleston, S. J. (1981), op. cit., pp. 334-5.
13 Quoted in Ibid, p. 335-336.
14 Adapted with substantial changes from California State Department of Education, *Planning for Multicultural Education as Part of School Improvement*, Sacramento, California: Superintendent of Public Instruction, 1979, p. 26.

Select bibliography

ALCOCK, A., et al., *The future of cultural minorities*, Macmillan, 1979.

ANWAR, M., *The myth of return: Pakistanis in Britain*, Heinemann Educational, 1979.

ARCINIEGA, T. A., 'The Challenge of Multicultural Education for Teacher Education', *Journal of Research and Development in Education* (1977), 11:1, pp. 52-69.

ATKINS, E., *Immigration and Racialism/(Labour Party)*, Labour Party, 1977.

BAGLEY, C., *A Comparative Perspective on the Education of Black Children in Britain*, Manchester: Centre for Educational Disadvantage, 1978.

BAGLEY, C., and VERMA, G. K., 'Development, norms and factorial validity for measuring racial attitudes in adolescents in multi-ethnic settings', *Educational Studies*, 4, no. 3, October 1978, pp. 189-200.

BAGLEY, C., *Racial prejudice*, Farnborough: Saxon House, 1979.

BAGLEY, C., and VERMA, G. K., 'Structure and relationship of self-esteem measured between ethnic groups and across culture'.

BANKS, J. A. and GRAMBE, J. D., *Black Self Concept*, (Implication for Education and Social Science), New York: McGraw Hill, 1972.

BELL, R., and GRANT, N., *Patterns of Education in the British Isles*, Allen and Unwin, 1977.

VAN DEN BERGHE, P. L., *Race and Racism (A Comparative Perspective)*, New York: John Wiley and Sons Inc., 1967.

VAN DEN BERGHE, P. L., *The Ethnic Phenomenon*, New York: Elsevier, 1981.

BHATNAGAR, J., *Immigrants at School*, Cornmarket Press, 1970.

BIDWELL, S., *Red, White and Black: race relations in Britain*, Gordon and Cremanion, 1976.

BLACK PEOPLE'S PROGRESSIVE ASSOCIATION, *Cause for Concern: West Indian pupils in Redbridge*, Black People's Progressive Association, Redbridge Community RelationsCouncil, Ilford: The Association, The Council, 1978.

BLAKELEY, M., 'Multiracial education: a positive approach', *Primary Education Review*, No. 8, Spring 1980, pp. 6-7.

BOLTON, E., 'Education in a multiracial society', *Trends Education*, no. 4, Winter 1979, pp. 3-7.

BOWKER, G., and CARRIER, J., *Race and ethnic relations: sociological readings*, Hutchinson, 1976.

BRITTAN, E., 'In-Service education and multiracial education', *British Journal of In-Service Education*, 5, no. 3, summer 1979, pp. 8-10.

BRITTAN, E. M., 'Teacher opinion on aspects of school life. Part 1: Changes in curriculum and school organization', *Educational Research*, 18, February, 1976, pp. 96-107.

BRITTAN, E., 'Teacher opinion on aspects of school life. Part 2: Pupils and teachers', *Educational Research*, 18 June 1976, pp. 182-191.

CAMERON, J., *Unemployment in Southall: a Report*, published for National Association for Asian Youth by Scope Communication, 1981.

CAMPBELL-PLATT, K., *Ethnic Minorities in Society: a Reference Guide*, CRRU of BCC and Runnymede Trust, 1976.

CARTER. D. E.. et al., 'Interracial acceptance in the classroom', in Foot, H. C., et al., eds., *Friendship and social relations in children*, Wiley, 1980, pp. 117-143.

CASHMORE. E.. *Rastaman*, Allen and Unwin, 1979.

CENTRE FOR APPLIED LINGUISTICS. *Bilingual Education: Current Perspectives*, Arlington, Virginia: Centre for Applied Linguistics, 1977.

CHASE. L. A.. *Let the Little Flowers Bloom (Race Relations, GB)*, Methodist Church Div. of Education and Youth, 1980.

COMMISSION FOR RACIAL EQUALITY. *Ethnic minority youth unemployment*: a paper presented to Government July 1980.

COMMISSION FOR RACIAL EQUALITY. Schools and Ethnic Minorities: comments on *Education in schools, a consultative document* by the DES.

COMMISSION FOR RACIAL EQUALITY. *Teacher education for a multicultural society*, CRE, 1978.

COMMUNITY RELATIONS COMMISSION, Reference and Technical Services Division, *The education of ethnic minority children: from the perspectives of parents, teachers and education authorities*, CRC, 1977.

COMMUNITY RELATIONS COMMISSION. *The Multi-racial Community: a guide for local councillors*, CRC, 1977.

COMMUNITY RELATIONS COMMISSION. *Review of the Race Relations Act*, CRC, 1975.

COMMUNITY RELATIONS COMMISSION. *A Second Chance: further education in multiracial areas*, Commission, Reference and Technical Services Division, 1976.

COMMUNITY RELATIONS COMMISSION. *Urban deprivation, racial inequality and social policy: a report*, HMSO, 1977.

CRAFT. M.. *Teaching in a Multicultural Society: The Task for Teacher Education*, Falmer Press, 1981.

CRAFT. M.. 'Education For Diversity: The Challenge of Cultural Pluralism' (Inaugural Lecture), University of Nottingham, 1982.

CRISHNA. S.. *Girls of Asian Origin in Britain*, YWCA of Great Britain.

CROSS. C.. *Ethnic Minorities in the inner city: the ethnic dimensions in urban deprivation in England*, CRE, 1978.

DAVEY. A.. 'Racial awareness in children and teacher education', *Education for Teaching*, no. 97, summer, 1975, pp. 25-33.

DEPARTMENT OF EDUCATION AND SCIENCE. *Potential and Progress in a Second Culture*, HMSO, 1971.

DEPARTMENT OF EDUCATION AND SCIENCE. *The Education of Immigrants*, HMSO, 1971.

DEPARTMENT OF EDUCATION AND SCIENCE. *The Continuing Needs of Immigrants*, HMSO, 1972.

DEPARTMENT OF EDUCATION AND SCIENCE. *Educational Disadvantage and the Educational Needs of Immigrants*, HMSO, 1974.

DEPARTMENT OF EDUCATION AND SCIENCE. *A Language for Life (The Bullock Report)*, HMSO, 1975.

DEPARTMENT OF EDUCATION AND SCIENCE. *Education in Schools: A Consultative Document*, HMSO, 1977.

DEPARTMENT OF EDUCATION AND SCIENCE. *Primary Education in England*, HMSO, 1978.

DEPARTMENT OF EDUCATION AND SCIENCE. *Aspects of Secondary Education in England*, HMSO, 1979.

DEPARTMENT OF EDUCATION AND SCIENCE. *The School Curriculum*, HMSO, 1981.

DEPARTMENT OF EDUCATION AND SCIENCE. *West Indian Children in Our Schools (The Rampton Report)*, HMSO, 1981.

DEPARTMENT OF EDUCATION AND SCIENCE. *Aspects of Organisation and Curriculum in Seven Multiethnic Comprehensive Schools*, A Report by HM Inspectors, 1981?

DICKINSON. L.. *The immigrant school learner: a study of Pakistani pupils in Glasgow*, for the Jordanhill College of Education, Slough: NFER, 1975.

DRIVER, G., Ethnicity and cultural competence: aspects of interaction in multiracial classrooms, *CORE*, 4, no. 1, March 1980.

D'SOUZE, M. B., 'Intergroup attitudes in Multi-ethnic schools', *Oxford Review of Education*, 4, no. 2, June 1978, pp. 149-160.

DUMMETT, A., *Citizenship and nationality*, with a foreword by J. E. S. Fawcett, Runnymede Trust, 1976.

DUNN, L. C., *Race, Science and Society*, Paris: UNESCO Press; London: Allen and Unwin, 1975.

EAST LONDON WORKERS AGAINST RACISM, *Our Flag Stays Red*, Revolutionary Communist Pamphlet no. 9, 1981.

EDDINGTON, D., 'Education for a Multi-racial Society', Schools Council Project, *Spectrum*, 7, no. 3, May 1975, pp. 7-8.

EDUCATION DIGEST, 'Multi-racial schools', *Education*, 148: 26 November 1976, p. i-iv.

EDWARDS, V., *West Indian Language: attitudes and the school*, Slough: National Association for Multiracial Education, 1976.

EDWARDS, V., *West Indian Language: attitudes and the school*, Revised ed: Derby: National Association for Multiracial Education, 1977.

EGGLESTON, S. J., et al., *In-Service Teacher Education in a Multicultural Soceity*, Keele: Univeristy of Keele, 1981, mimeo.

FARLEY, C.,'Teaching soical studies in a school with a large ethnic minority', *Social Science Teacher*, 9, no. 3, February 1980, pp. 86-87.

FILE, N., *Black settlers in Britain 1555 - 1958*, Heinemann Educational, 1981.

FISHER, G., 'Ethnic Minorities: beyond "Yellow Bird"', *Music in Education*, 42, no. 395, July 1978, pp. 284-286.

FISHMAN, J., *Bilingual Education*, Rawley, Mass: Newbury House, 1976.

FONER, N., *Jamaica farewell: Jamaica Migrants in London*, Routledge and Kegan Paul, 1979.

FRAENKEL, J., *The History of the British Section of the World Jewish Congress*, 1977.

GARCIA, R. L., *Fostering a Pluralistic Society through Multi-Ethnic Education*, Bloomington, Indiana: Phil Delta Kappa Educational Foundation, 1978.

GARVIE, E., 'What's in a name?', *Times Educational Supplement*, no. 3273, 17 March 1978, p. 19.

GHUMAN, P. A. S., *The Cultural Content of thinking: a comparative study of Punjabi and English boys*, Windsor: NFER, 1975.

GILES, R. and CHERRINGTON, D. *Multicultural Education in the UK: A Survey of Courses and other Provision in British Institutions of Higher Education*, CRE, 1981, unpublished.

GILL, M., and GILL, D., 'Multicultural Maths', *Maths in School*, 6, no. 2, March 1977, pp. 6-9.

GILROY, B., *Black Teacher*, Cassell, 1976.

GLAZER, N., *Affirmative Discrimination* (Ethnic Inequality and Public Policy), New York: Basic Books Inc., 1975.

GLAZER, N., and MOYNIHAN, D. P., *Ethnicity, (Theory and Experience)*, Cambridge, Mass: Harvard University Press, 1975.

GLAZER, N., and MOYNIHAN, D. P., *Beyond the Melting Pot*, Cambridge, Mass: The Uni Press, 1963 (Second edition 1970).

GOEL, K. M., *Growth of immigrant children in Glasgow*, Oxfam, 1980.

GOODY, J., 'Classroom interaction in the multi-racial school', *English in Education*, 11, no. 1: Spring 1977, pp. 2-10

GORDON, M. M., *Assimilation in American Life*, New York: Oxford University Press, 1964.

GRANT, C. A., 'Education that is multicultural and urban schools: rationale and recommendations', *British Journal of In-Service Education*, 6, no. 2, Spring 1980, pp. 69-78.

GRANT, C. A., *Multiracial Education: Commitments, Issues and Applications*,

Association for Supervision and Curriculum Development, 1977.

GILES, R. H., *The West Indian experience in British schools: multiracial education and social disadvantage in London*, Heinemann Educational, 1977.

GWINNETT, D., 'Music in a Multi-cultural School', *Music Teacher*, 58, no. 9, September 1979, pp. 13-15.

HALEY, F., et al., *Ethnic Studies Handbook for School Librarians*, Boulder, Colorado: Social Science Education Consortium Inc., 1978.

HAMALIAN, A., 'National integration in multiethnic societies: the differential role of schooling and non-formal education', *Compare*, 9, no. 1, April 1979, pp. 33-44.

HAMNETT, C., 'Multiple deprivation and the Inner City', *Immigrants and inequality*, by Peter Braham for the O.U. Course Team, Milton Keynes: O.U.P., 1976.

HANKS, B. C., 'Towards Multicultural understanding 2: the mulitracial school', *Trends in Education*, September 1975, pp. 10-14.

HANSEN-KRENING, N., *Competency and Creativity in Language Arts: A Multiethnic Focus*, Reading, Mass: Addison-Wesley Publishing Company, 1979.

HICKS, D., 'Two sides of the same coin: development education, multicultural education', *New Era*, 60, no. 2, March-April 1979, pp. 55-61.

HILL, D., *Teaching in Multiracial Schools: a Guidebook*, Methuen, 1976.

The History and Social Science Teacher (1981), Vol. 17, No. 1, (Fall 1981), Special issue on Multiculturalism.

HOLMES, B., *Diversity and Unity in Education*, Allen and Unwin, 1980.

HOLMES, C.

HOME OFFICE, *Social Discrimination*, HMSO, 1975.

HOME OFFICE, *Racial Discrimination: a guide to the Race Relations Act, 1976*, HMSO, 1977.

HOPKINS, A., 'If it doesn't happen in Liverpool..', *T.E.S.*, no. 3235, 3 June 1977, pp. 18-19.

HOUSE OF COMMONS, HOME AFFAIRS COMMITTEE, *Racial Discrimination. Fifth Report from the Home Affairs Committee*, Session 1980-81: HMSO.

HOUSE OF COMMONS, HOME AFFAIRS COMMITTEE, *The Operation and Effectiveness of the Commission for Racial Equality*, Session 1980-81: HMSO, 1981.

HUBBUCK, J., and CARTER, S. E., *Half a Chance?: a report on job discrimination against young blacks in Nottingham*, CRE, 1980.

IVATTS, A. R., *'Catch 22 Gypsies'*, Advisory Committee for the Education of Romany and other Travellers, 1975.

JACKSON, B., *Starting School*, Croom Helm, 1979.

JAMES, A., 'Cheating a philosophy', *T.E.S.*, no. 3208, 26 November 1976, p. 21.

JAMES, A., 'Education for a Multicultural Society: Aims for Primary and Middle Schools', *Education 3-13*, vol. 9, no. 1, Spring 1981.

JAY, E., *Racial Discrimination*, S.C.M. Press for Christian Education Movement, 1971.

JEFFCOATE, R., Curriculum planning in multiracial education, *Educational Research*, 18 June 1976, pp. 192-200.

JEFFCOATE, R., 'A multicultural curriculum: beyond the orthodoxy', *Trends in Education*, no. 4, Winter 1979, pp. 8-12.

JEFFCOATE, R., *Positive image: towards a multicultural curriculum*, Writers and Readers Publishing Cooperative for Chameleon, 1979.

JEFFCOATE, R., 'Towards multicultural understanding: 1 Schools and prejudice', *Trends in Education*, September, 1975, pp. 3-5.

JEFFCOATE, R., 'Why multicultural education', *Education 3-13*, vol. 9, no. 1, Spring 1981.

JELINEK, M., and BRITTAN, E.M., 'Multiracial education, 1: Interethnic friendship patterns,' *Educational Research*, 18, November 1975, pp. 44-53.

JELINEK, M. M., 'Pupil's attitudes to the multi-racial school', *Educational Research*, 3, 19 February 1977, pp. 129-141.

KANNAN, C. T., *Cultural Adaptation of Asian immigrants: first and second generation,* C. T. Kannan, 1978.

KAPO, R., *A Savage Culture,* (Race Relations, G.B.), Quartet, 1981.

KHAN, V. S., *Bilingual and linguistic Minorities in Britain: developments, perspectives,* Runnymede Trust, 1978.

KHAN, V. S. (ed.), *Minority families in Britain: support and stress,* Macmillan, 1979.

KING, E. W., *The Complete Handbook for Multiethnic Education: Grades K-6,* Santa Monica, California: Goodyear Publishing Company, 1980.

KIRKWOOD, K., 'Ethnic, cultural and racial pluralism: awareness, education and policy', *Oxford Review of Education,* 1, 1975, pp. 107-16.

KOHLER, D. F., *Ethnic Minorities in Britain: Statistical Data,* Community Relations Commission, 1975.

KOHLER, D. F., *Ethnic Minorities in Britain: Statistical Data—5th ed.,* CRC, 1975.

LANDIS, D., and McGREW, P., 'Subjective culture and the perceptions of black and white urban school teachers'. In VERMA, G.K., and BAGLEY, C., eds., *Race, education and identity,* Macmillan, 1979, pp. 51-63.

LASHLEY, H., 'Race, unemployment and F.E.', *Liberal Education,* no. 37, Spring, 1979, pp. 12-15.

LENNOX COOK, J., *A new way to proficiency in English: a comprehensive guide to English as a foreign language,* Blackwell, 1980.

LEWIS, E. G., *Bilingualism and Bilingual Education: A Comparative Study,* University of New Mexico Press, 1980.

LEWIS, T., 'Ethnic influences on girls' P.E.', *British Journal of Physical Education,* 10, no. 5, September 1979, p. 132.

LINDEN, G., 'Teaching history in a multi-ethnic high school', *Teaching History,* 4, May 1976, pp. 244-249.

LUDUS NORTH WEST DANCE IN EDUCATION, *Suggestions for multicultural education: a practical teaching guide/Ludus North West Dance in Education,* Lancaster: Ludus North West Dance in Education, 1979.

LUNN, K., (ed.), *Hosts, immigrants and minorities: historical responses to newcomers in British society, 1870-1914,* Dawson, 1980.

LUSTGARTEN, L., *Legal control of racial discrimination,* Macmillan, 1980.

LYNCH, J., 'Training bi-lingual teachers for the multi-racial society', *International Review of Education,* 24, no. 3, 1978, pp. 393-395.

MACDONALD, I. A., *Race Relations: the new law,* Butterworth, 1977.

McDERMOTT, R. P., and GOSPODINOFF, K., 'Social contexts for ethnic borders and school failure', In Wolfgang, A. (ed.), *Non-verbal behaviour,* pp. 175-195.

MACKILLOP, J., *Ethnic Minorities in Sheffield,* City of Sheffield Adult Education Department, 1981.

McLEAN, M., 'Cultural autonomy and the education of ethnic minority groups', *British Journal of Education Studies,* 28, no. 1, February 1980, pp. 9-12.

MANTERO, D., *Japanese Americans: Changing Patterns of Ethnic Affiliations over three Generations,* Boulder, Colorado: Westview Press, 1980.

MARJORIBANKS, K., *Ethnic families and children's achievements*, Allen and Unwin, 1980.

MILES, R., *Between two cultures?: the case of Rastafarianism*, University of Bristol, SSRC Research Unit on Ethnic Relations, 1978.

MILNER, D., *Children and Race*, Harmondsworth: Penguin, 1975.

MOBBS, M. C., *Meeting their needs: an account of the language tuition schemes for ethnic minority women*, Community Relations Commission, 1977.

MOON, J., and REID, D., 'Some considerations in social policy for the under-fives in a multiracial Britain', *Early Child Development Care,* 6, nos 1/2, 1979, pp. 45-59.

MUBBUCK, J., and CARTER, S., *Half a chance?: a report on job discrimination against young blacks in Nottingham,* Commission for Racial Equality in association with Nottingham and District Community Relations Council, 1980.

NATIONAL ASSOCIATION OF MULTIRACIAL EDUCATION, 'New Approaches in Multiracial Education', *Journal of the National Association for Multiracial Education*, Autumn 1978, vol. 7, no. 1.

NATIONAL ASSOCIATION FOR THE TEACHING OF ENGLISH, 'The teaching of English in multicultural Britain: a discussion document', N.A.T.E., 1979.

NATIONAL CATHOLIC COMMISSION FOR RACIAL JUSTICE, *Where Creed and Colour Matter: a survey on black children and Catholic schools*, Abbots Langley: NCCRJ, 1975.

NATIONAL STUDY OF SCHOOL EVALUATION, *Evaluation Guidelines for Multicultural-Multiracial Education*, Arlington, Va: National Study of School Education, 1973.

NTUK-IDEM, M. J., *Compensatory Education*, Farnborough, Hants: Saxon House, July 1978.

O'CONNOR, E., and TAMES, R., 'Teach history in a Multi-racial Society', *Trends in Education,* no. 1, Spring 1978, pp. 25-31.

PARSONS, D., 'Education in a multi-racial society', *Secondary Education,* 5, June 1975, pp. 39-41.

PEARSON, D., *Race, class and political ativism: a study of West Indians in Britain*, Gower, 1981.

PORTER, J., 'To reduce the ignorance upon which stereotypes feed is becoming an increasingly urgent matter', *T.E.S.*, no. 3328, 21 March, 1980, p. 21.

PRYCE, K., *Endless pressure: a study of West Indian life-styles in Bristol*, Harmondsworth: Penguin, 1979.

RACE RELATIONS COMMISSION, *Education of ethnic minorities: comments on the consultative document issued by the DES on the Report on the West Indian Community issued by the Select Committee on Race Relations and Immigration*, The Commission, 1977.

RACE RELATIONS BOARD, *Report of the Race Relations Board*, HMSO, 1975-76.

RATCLIFFE, P., *Racism and Reaction*, Race Relations, Birmingham, Harmondsworth, RKP, 1981.

REX, J., *Colonial immigrants in a British city*, Routledge and Kegan Paul, 1979.

RICHARDS, J. K., 'More than two cultures', *T.E.S.*, no. 3261, 9 December 1977, p. 25.

RICHMOND, W. K., *Education in Britain since 1944: a personal report*, Methuen, 1978.

ROBINSON, V., *The Dynamics of Ethnic Succession: a British case study, (Housing Segregation-Blackburn)*, University of Oxford School of Geography.

ROWE, A., 'The Outsiders', *T.E.S.*, no. 3340, 20 June 1980, p. 4.

ROVARETTI, J. V., 'Ethnic Minority group children in the primary school', *Education for Development*, 4, no. 4, October 1977, pp. 34-39.

RUNNYMEDE TRUST and RADICAL STATISTICS, *Britain's black population*, Heinemann Educational, 1980.

RUSHTON, J., and TURNER, J. D., *Education and deprivation*, Manchester: Manchester University Press, 1975.

SAUNDERS, M., *Multicultural Teaching,* McGraw-Hill, 1982.

SCHOOLS COUNCIL, 'Race and teachers: the Schools Council study', *New Society*, 43, no. 802, 16 February 1978, pp. 366-368.

SHUKLA, H., 'Minority ethnic groups: the needs of the children', *AREA*, 11, Bull. 27 and 28: 1978, pp. 15-18.

SIBLEY, D., *Outsiders in Urban Society*, B. Blackwell, 1981.

SIKES, P. D. and SHEARD, D. S., 'Teaching for better race relations?', *Cambridge Journal of Education*, 8, nos. 2-3, 1978, pp. 165-172.

SIMOES, A., *The Bilingual Child: research and analysis of existing educational themes*, New York; London: Academic Press, 1976.

SMITH, D. G., *Racial disadvantage in Britain: the P.E.P. report*, Harmondsworth: Penguin, 1977.

SMITH, D. J., *The facts of racial disadvantage: a national survey*, P.E.P., 1976.

SMITH, L. A., (ed.), *Education in a Multi-cultural Society: report on a one-day conference arranged by the School of Education, Goldsmiths' College*, The College 1980.

SOUTHALL (LONDON BOROUGH OF), *The Birth of a Black Community (Race Relations 1950-81)*, (Campaign Against Racism and Fascism Viewpoints), Institute of Race Relations, 1981.

STEWART, P., *Immigrants*, Batsford, 1976.

STOCK, A. K., and HOWELL, D., *Education for Adult Immigrants*, Leicester: National Institute of Adult Education, 1976.

STONE, M., *The Education of the Black Child in Britain: the myth of multiracial education*, Fontana, 1981.

STONES, E., 'The colour of conceptual learning', in VERMA, G. K., and BAGLEY, C., (eds.), *Race, Education and Identity*, Macmillan, 1979, pp. 67-83.

STREET-PORTER, R., *Race, Children and Cities*, Open University Press, 1978, E361, Block 5.

SUTHERLAND, M. B., 'Comparative perspectives on the education of cultural minorities', in ALCOCK, A. E., et al., (eds.), *The future of cultural minorities*, Macmillan, 1979, pp. 44-62.

TAMBS-LYCHG, M., *London Patidars: a case study in urban ethnicity*, Routledge and Kegan Paul, 1980.

TAYLOR, J. H., *The half-way generation: a study of Asian Youths in Newcastle upon Tyne*, Windsor: NFER, 1976.

THOMAS, K. C., 'Colour of tester effects on children's expressed attitudes', *British Educational Research Journal*, 4, October 1978, pp. 83-90.

THOMSON, G., *Race Relations*, Glasgow: Blackie, 1977.

TOMLINSON, S., 'Multiracial schooling: parents' and teachers' views', *Education 3-13*, vol. 9, no. 1, Spring 1981.

TROYNA, B. S., 'Race and streaming: a case study', *Educational Review*, 30, no. 1, February 1978, pp. 59-65.

UNITED STATES COMMISSION ON CIVIL RIGHTS, *Affirmative Action in the 1980s. Dismantling the Process of Discrimination*, Washington DC 20425: US Commission of Civil Rights, 1981.

UNITED STATES COMMISSION ON CIVIL RIGHTS, *A Better Chance to Learn: Bilingual-Bicultural Education*, Washington DC: United States Government Printing Office, 1975, (US Commission on Civil Rights Clearing House Publication No. 51).

UNIVERSITY OF IBADAN, DEPARTMENT OF SOCIOLOGY, *Report of a Seminar on 'The African Child in Great Britain', Ibadan, Nigeria, 1-13 March 1975*, Commonwealth Students' Children Society, Department of Sociology, University of Ibadan, 1976.

VERMA, G. K., and MALLICK, K., 'The growth and nature of self-esteem: attitudes and feelings in multi-ethnic schools', *New Era*, 59, no. 4, July-August 1978, pp. 150-154.

VERMA, G. K., and BAGLEY, C., *Race and Education Across Cultures*, Heinemann Educational, 1975.

VERMA, G. K., and BAGLEY, C., eds., *Race, Education and Identity*, Macmillan, 1979.

VERMA, G. K., and BAGLEY, C., 'Teaching styles and race relations: some effects on white teenagers', *New Era*, no. 2, March-April, 1978, pp. 53-57.

WAINWRIGHT, D. F., 'Ethnic Minorities: music for the multi-cultural school', *Music in Education*, 42, no. 392, April 1978, pp. 158-160.

WARNOCK, M., 'Cultural relativism and education', *Westminster Studies in Education*, 2, November 1979, pp. 35-44.

WATSON, J. L., *Between two cultures: migrants and minorities in Britain*, Oxford: Blackwell, 1977.

WATSON, K., 'Educational policies in multi-cultural societies', *Comparative Education*, 15, no. 1, March 1979, pp. 17-31.

WILLEY, R., 'Teacher education for a multi-racial society', *New Era*, 56, April 1975, pp. 76-78.

WILLEY, R., 'Teacher education for a multi-cultural society', *Education for teaching*, no. 97, Summer 1975, pp. 34-39.

WINKLEY, D., 'Multicultural policy and practice: a view from Grove Junior School', *Education 3-13,* vol. 9, no. 1, Spring 1981.

WOLFGANG, A., 'The teacher and nonverbal behaviour in the multicultural classroom', in WOLFGANG, A., (ed.), *Nonverbal behaviour,* Academic Press, 1979, pp. 159-174.

WORRALL, M., 'Multiracial Britain and the third world: tensions and approaches in the classroom', *New Era,* 59, no. 2, March-April, 1978, pp. 47-52.

Index

accountability, 22, 81, 114
achievement, 28, 43, 78, 87
activity method: teaching, 39
American Association of
    Colleges for Teacher
    Education, 114
Archambault, R.D., 135
*Aspects of Organisation and
    Curriculum in Seven
    Multiethnic Comprehensive
    Schools,* (1979), 87, 137, 143
Assessment of Performance Unit
    (DES), 72
assimilation: cultural groups, 24,
    25
Aston, A., 133
Australia, 113
    core learning, 52 (fig.)
    curriculum courses, 49
    Curriculum Development
        Centre, 51, 63
    New South Wales Department
        of Education, 139
    polyethnic curriculum, 48
    Schools Commission, 139
    teacher education, 139
Australian Institute of
    Multicultural Affairs, 111,
    139
Avon Education Department, 90

Bagley, C., 46, 132, 137
Baker, K.A., 142
Banks, C.A.M., 132

Banks, J.A., 30, 32, 47, 49, 113,
    132, 133, 134, 140
Bantock, G.H. 77, 136
Barnes, D., 116, 132, 141
Becher, T., 131, 136
Bedford Language Project, 46
Benjamin, H., 130
Bennett, N., 86
bilingual education, 116
Bindman, G., 115, 141
Biott, C., 131, 136
Birley High School
        (Manchester), 45, 94, 114,
        134, 138, 141
    multicultural curriculum, 51,
        53
Black Studies Curriculum, 44
Bradford Language Project, 46,
    116, 141
Bradford Metropolitan District,
    45
Brent, London Borough of, 19,
    131, 138, 141
    multicultural education in, 92,
    114
    Teachers' Association, 57
Bristol Council for Racial
Equality, 90
Brittan, E.M., 115, 133, 135
Bruner, J., 27, 59, 113, 132, 134,
    136
Bullivant, B.M., 12, 48, 76, 77,
    113, 130, 134, 136, 140
Bullock Report (1975), 85-6, 137
Bulmershe College of Higher
    Education (Reading), 103

Candlin, C., 141
Canada, 96
Carrington, B., 78, 136
Central Advisory Council for
    Education, 137
Centre for Applied Research in
    Education, 36, 113, 140
Centre for Information on
    Language Teaching (CILT),
    117
Centre for Urban Educational
    Studies (CUES), 112, 140
Children's Right Workshop, 112,
    139
Circular 6/81 (DES), 108, 120
Claydon, L., 140
Coard, B., 136
Cole, M., 136
Commission for Racial Equality,
    90, 107, 128
    publications, 112, 114, 116,
    117, 136, 139, 140
Commonwealth Institute, 117,
    142
community learning resources
    consultant, 96
community resources, 104-5,
    and staff development, 106-7
compensatory education, 43
'cone experience', 75
conscientization, 93
*Core Curriculum for Australian
    Schools* (1980), 63-4, 73
Craft, M., 91, 114, 138, 140
culture
    defined, 13
    differences, 33, 34, 42
    pluralism, 26, 42, 70
    United States, 41, 42
    transmission, 11-12
Curriculum Development Centre
    (Australia), 51, 63, 134, 135
Curriculum 11-16 (1977), 72-3,
    135
curriculum reform, 50 (fig.)

Dale, E., 75, 135
De Kanter, A.A., 142
Denuth, C., 134, 138
Department of Education and
    Science, 136, 137
Derrick, J., 116, 141
discourse, 20, 84, 89-90
    role of, 22
discrimination, 32-3, 43, 99, 114,
    119-20
discussion method: teaching, 27,
    36, 37
Downing, J., 132
D'Oyley, V., 138
drama, improvised: teaching
    methods, 37
Driver, D., 136
Driver, G., 137
Dummett, A., 134

Ealing Community Relations
    Council, 89, 137
Education Act 1980, 87, 108, 137
education, aims of, 60-68
*Education for a Multiracial
    Society* (1981), 45, 46, 65, 67,
    93, 112
*Education in Schools: a
    Consultative Document*
    (1977), 61-2, 134
*Education of Children from
    Ethnic Minority Groups*
    (1982), 58
Educational Research
    Information Centre (ERIC),
    111
Edwards, V., 116, 141
Eggleston, S.J., 114, 122, 139,
    140, 142, 143
Eisner, E., 135
Elkin, J., 112, 139
Elliott, G., 131
Elliott, J., 114, 136, 140
emancipatory education, 32, 35
enculturation, 13

English, 70, 94,
  as a second language, 94, 116
equality of opportunity, 15, 26,
    78, 80
  United States, 41
Ethnic Heritage Studies
    Program, 29, 41, 132, 139
ethnic identity, 32, 39
ethnic studies, 50 (fig.)
evaluation, 14, 15, 58, 82
  criteria, 16, 80
  United States, 81-2

Fitzpatrick, F., 141, 142
Flynn, J.R., 115, 141
Freire, P., 93
Further Education Research and
    Development Unit (DES),
    113, 135, 140

Gagné, R.M., 75, 136
Garcia, R.L., 39, 133
Garvie, E., 116, 141
Gibson, M.A., 41, 43, 133
Giles, R., 136
Gordon, N.M., 25, 131
Gould, J., 130
government policy, suggestions
    for, 119-23
Grant, G., 39, 133
Green, P., 132
group work: teaching methods,
    31

Habermas, J., 72, 94, 131, 135,
    138
Hall, S., 33, 133
Hall, S.J., 132
Hamilton, D., 114, 140
Hammersley, M., 137
Hansen-Krening, N., 39, 133
Hanson, L., 134
Hargreaves, D., 90, 137
Haringey Reading Project, 97
Herbart, J.F., 91

Hewison, J., 138
Hicks, D., 112, 132, 139
hidden curriculum, 28
Hills, K., 138
Hirst, P.H., 13, 130, 135
Home Office, 141, 142
home—school relations, 59, 85,
    105, 110
home tuition schemes, 94
Hooper, R., 130
House of Commons, Home
    Affairs Committee, 44, 88,
    133, 137, 138, 141
House of Commons Select
    Committee on Race
    Relations and Immigration,
    115, 141
Houston, J., 132
Humanities Curriculum Project,
    35, 36-7, 45, 113

imagination, 93
information bank, 103
  concepts, 43
information sources, 111-16
Inner London Education
    Authority, 136, 137
  Centre for Learning
    Resources, 106
  guidelines, 114, 141
  Learning Materials Services,
    117, 141
  Multiethnic Inspectorate, 27,
    80
in-service courses, 107-8, 122-3,
    126
*In-service Teacher Education in
    a Multiracial Society* (1981),
    126
Institute of Race Relations, 117

James, A., 130, 140
Jeffcoate, R., 13, 15, 20, 27, 28,
    47, 115, 130, 131, 132, 134,
    140, 141

Jones, C., 132

Kahn, N., 136
Khan, V.S., 46, 142
King, E.W., 39, 133
Klein, G., 103, 111, 132, 139
knowledge chart, 21, 70
knowledge selection, 13, 14
  social criteria, 17 (fig.), 19, 20
Kolb, W.L., 130

Lacey, C., 131, 136
Lambeth Whole School Project,
  90
Lawton, D., 114, 131, 134, 135,
  136, 140
Leach, E., 14, 130
Lee, M., 141
Leicester Council for
    Community Relations, 138
Leicestershire County Council,
  91
Lester, A., 115, 141
library organisation, 108-10
Little, A., 45, 46, 134, 138, 141
Lorac, C., 135, 140
Lynch, J., 44, 112, 130, 131, 133,
  137, 138, 139

McDiarmid, G., 132
MacDonald, B., 114, 132, 136,
  140
MacKillop, J., 138
Maclure, S., 136
Mallea, J.R., 114, 140
Man A Course of Study
    (MACOS), 113
Marjoribanks, K., 135
Maryland State Department of
    Education, 136
Matthews, A., 122, 139, 142
Maxwell, J., 140
Merton, London Borough of, 92
Miller, H. J., 133
Milner, D., 114

moral development, 14, 43
Morrish, I., 113, 140
mother-tongue, 44, 70, 116
  teaching and learning, 70, 95
motivation, 78
multicultural curriculum, 43,
  46-8
  construction, 56 (fig.)
  development, 122
multicultural education, 15, 40,
  129
  aims of, 49, 60-8
  objectives, 66 (fig.)
  policy, 121
  school research in, 100
Multicultural Education (1982),
  65, 66 (fig.), 70, 140
multiracial curriculum, 47-8
multiracial society, 9-10
Mulvaney, M., 130
Musgrave, P.W., 71, 135

National Association for
    Multiracial Education, 95,
    103, 112, 117, 139
  courses, 107
  publications, 138
National Association for Race
    Relations and Action
    Research, 37
National Association for
    Teaching English as a
    Second Language to Adults,
    138
National Association of
    Teachers in Colleges of
    Further and Higher
    Education, 114
National Committee on Racism
    in Children's Books, 112,
    139
National Council for the Social
    Studies, 81, 136
National Education Association
    (USA), 81, 136

National Study of School Evaluation (1973), 81, 136
National Union of Teachers (NUT), 115, 116
  course provision, 107
  publications, 132, 137, 141, 142
Newsom Report (1963), 84, 137
Nuttall, D.L., 137, 139

Ogbu, J., 137
open classrooms, 27, 104
  construction of, 53,
  cultural participation in, 31,
  principles of, 35
organisations, 85, 103, 107, 111, 117

Parekh, B., 93, 138
parent participation, 88, 91, 95, 97
Parents and Teachers (1976), 85
Paton, H.J., 131
Peters, R.S., 13, 14, 55, 130, 131, 134
Phillips, D., 131
Pimlott, J., 137
Plowden Report (1967), 85
pluralism, 12, 49, 99
  cultural aspects, 26, 42
polyethnic curriculum, 48
Practical Curriculum (1981), 22, 96
Pratt, D., 132
Preston, M., 138
Price, C.A., 132
'Profile of Excellence' (USA), 81-2
'Purpose and Planning in Schools' (Schools Council), 82

race relations: teaching methods, 37-8
racial attitudes, 30-2
Racial Disadvantage (1982), 44, 88, 139, 141

racial prejudice, 28-32 *passim,* 43
Raising the School Leaving Age (1965), 36
Rampton Report (1981), 87-8, 126, 137
Rees, D.A., 141
research, 99-100
resource centres, 117
Resources Information Bank on Multicultural Education (RIBMESC), 103, 111
'respect for persons', 19, 20, 21, 55, 60
  as curriculum focus, 47-8
Rex, J., 46, 88, 137
Reynolds, J., 123, 140, 142
Richardson, A., 131
role reversal: teaching methods, 31
Rose, E.J.B., 114, 141
Rowley, G., 130
Rudduck, J., 36, 133
Runnymede Trust, 117, 130, 139, 140
  Radical Statistics Group, 113

sabre-tooth curriculum, 16
Salter, B., 131
school-community relations, 84-98, 106, 122
School Curriculum (1981), 18-19, 62, 63, 108, 131, 135
school, function of, 14
school objectives, 124-5
school resource centres, 106
  library organisation, 109-10
Schools Council, 82, 112
  publications, 113, 131-40 *passim,* 143
Scrimshaw, P., 124, 142
Searle, C., 116, 141
self-concept, 28, 43
Shea, E.C., 114, 140
Sikes, P., 133
Simons, H., 136

situational analysis, 123
Skilbeck, M., 114, 123, 140, 142
Smith, E., 141
Smolicz, J.J., 49, 134
social relationships, 27-8
social skills, 67
society, values in, 64
Sockett, H., 136
Sowell, T., 132
staff development, 102, 105-6,
    110-11, 122
Stenhouse, L., 30, 34, 35, 47, 114,
    123, 132, 133, 134, 135, 140,
    142
stereotyping, 26, 31, 32, 116
Stone, M., 78, 95, 136, 138
Sugarman, B., 131

Taft, R., 131
Tapper, T., 131
Tasmania: Education
    Department, 139
Tawney, D., 114, 140
Taylor, F., 112, 139
Taylor, M.J., 28, 132, 137, 139
Taylor Report (1977), 86, 137
teacher education
    information sources, 114
    multicultural curricula, 44,
        127 (fig.), 127-8
Teaching About Race Relations
    (1979), 37-8
teachers
    expectations, 28
    role of, 35
    self-evaluation, 22
    status, 96
    see also staff development
teaching, 126-8
    criteria, 79-80
    methods, 27, 31, 36, 37, 39
Todd, F., 116., 141
Tough, J., 116, 141

Townsend, H.E.R., 115, 133, 135,
    141
Twitchin, J., 134, 138

underachievement, *see*
    achievement
United Kingdom, 98
    as multicultural society, 9-10
United States, 41, 81, 113
    education departments, 142,
        143
    educational strategies, 41, 44
    multiethnic curriculum, 49-50
    racial attitudes, 30
    West Indian migrants, 28
University of East Anglia, 34, 35
    see also Centre for Applied
        Research in Education

value concepts, 12
Verma, G.K., 46, 132, 137
voluntary organisations, 117

Weiss, M., 135, 140
West Indian pupils, 28, 78
White, J.P., 62, 130, 131, 135
Whitehead, F., 116, 141
Wilding, J., 134
Willey, R., 45, 134, 138, 141
Williams, J., 43, 133
Williams, N., 131
Wilson, J., 20, 131
Woods, P., 137
World Council of Churches
        Workshop on Racism in
        Children's and School
        Textbooks, 29
Wright, L., 134

Young School Leavers, (1968),
    85

Zec, P., 14, 130